Ernest and Pauline trudged up a snow-covered slope.

They stopped briefly to strip the wet snow from their skis. A hot sun shone down from an azure sky, casting a sharp clear light on everything below.

"May I ask you something?" Pauline said. "You don't have to answer."

"Go ahead," said Ernest good-naturedly. "Shoot."

"What makes you happy?"

Ernest reflected for a moment. "Two private *Barrera* seats in a big bullfighting arena and a trout stream all to myself."

Pauline shook her head. "What else?"

"Oh, two charming houses in the city—one where I'd have my wife and childen, where I'd live monogamously and love them sincerely. And another one where I'd keep my beautiful mistresses on nine different floors."

"You're making fun of me." Annoyed, she pushed off and skied down the slope, followed by Ernest. Suddenly she disappeared behind a mound. He heard her cry out and hurried to her. She lay in the snow, one ski off and the other dangling. He knelt beside her and in a moment she was on her feet. She held him tightly.

"You're trembling," he said.

Pauline closed her eyes. Their faces came closer and closer. They kissed tenderly at first, cautiously, then more and more passionately.

"I love you," she whispered. "I love you."

HEMINGWAY

CHRISTOPHER COOK GILMORE

ST. MARTIN'S PRESS / New York

To Peter Miller, Superagent

Cover photographs courtesy of Daniel Wilson Productions, Inc. and Alcor Film

HEMINGWAY

Copyright © 1988 by Alcor Film Gmbh and Daniel Wilson Productions, Inc.

ISBN: 0-312-91175-0   Can. ISBN: 0-312-91176-9

Printed in the United States of America

First St. Martin's Press mass market edition/May 1988

10 9 8 7 6 5 4 3 2 1

PART

One

Fossalta, Italy—1918

Ernest Hemingway peered into the darkness as he pushed his bicycle along the muddy country path. Leaning into the wind, he felt his way through the familiar terrain until he came to the ruins of a stone farmhouse, a frontline command post where a dozen Italian soldiers waited for the next German attack. Wearily he leaned his bike against a wall, took a bag from his shoulder, and wordlessly began to pass out chocolate, cigarettes, and mail.

"Where do you come from, friend?" asked a soldier.

"Chicago."

"Chicago?" They all mouthed the word. "Chicago?"

"America," said Hemingway.

"America!" A sergeant laughed. "This is the farthest I've ever been from home, right here, the farthest yet. I come from the Abruzzi. I am fifty-five years old and all these years I have never been out of the Abruzzi."

"You're too old for this war, Dad," said Hemingway, who was eighteen.

The sergeant held up a finger. "Does that mean I cannot die like all the others?"

Suddenly they heard a whizzing sound coming closer and closer. For a second the men froze, then everyone scrambled for cover. With a tremendous explosion, a mortar round landed a few yards away, sending a rain of shrapnel, wooden splinters, stones, and

3

dirt through the night air. Men screamed as a wall collapsed on them. Another round fell and Hemingway was thrown to the ground, the wind knocked out of him. He tried to move but the body of a dead soldier pinned him to the ground. Running a free hand down his legs, he found his boots riddled with holes, blood seeping out of them. He pushed the corpse away, got to his knees, and looked around.

Badly wounded, a soldier screamed in pain. Laboriously, Ernest crawled to him, made it to his feet, and began to drag the soldier from under a heavy beam. Passing other dead and wounded, he slung the soldier over his back and started walking toward the nearest trench, some one hundred yards away. The man on his back was heavy. Ernest stumbled, almost fell. A salvo of machine-gun fire erupted from the opposite bank of the Piave River.

The soldiers in the trench watched the American volunteer walk out of the burning village, the wounded soldier still slung over his back. Hemingway was halfway there when another burst of heavy machine-gun fire erupted, hitting him in his right knee. He crashed to the ground, the wounded man falling on top of him. No one moved to help him.

Ernest gasped, reaching for his leg with his right hand. When he looked, it was covered with blood. He tried to get to his feet, but kept losing his footing.

"Oh God, help me! Help me out of here!"

He rolled the soldier onto his side and somehow struggled to his feet. He looked around, checked his position, then bent down and tried to hoist the soldier to his back. Gasping for air and gritting his teeth, he staggered forward. Trying with all his might and willpower just to put one foot before the other, he finally reached the trench where friendly hands pulled him to safety.

Hemingway caught a glimpse of the stars before he passed out.

Bay View, Michigan—Summer, 1921

The wedding guests were gathered under the large, shady elms. It was very hot. Restless, the guests waited for the bride. Grace Hemingway, Ernest's mother, was tense, nervous. His father, Dr. Hemingway, sweated profusely in his three-piece suit. He wiped his forehead with a handkerchief.

"Let's go on in, Grace. It's cooler inside. The guests are getting restless."

"Where is that girl?"

"God knows."

"Well, I'll never understand why Ernest insisted on getting married up here. After all, Oak Park would have been so much more convenient."

"Grace, Ernest spent the best years of his life here. Remember the summer parties? The hunting, the fishing, the Indians?"

"That's all very well. But I had to ask all our Chicago friends to make the long trip up here. Ernest never considers us."

"Yes, dear."

She looked nervously down the dusty country road. "She would be late! For her own wedding!"

Dr. Hemingway gently took his wife's arm and led her to the entrance to the church, where their son and some of his friends were standing. Ernest was practicing a little boxing footwork when he saw his bride-to-be walking up the road. Hadley, wearing a beige lace dress, was lovely. She handed her husband-to-be a wreath with her bridal veil. Taking her aside and looking deeply into her eyes, Hemingway ran his hand through her auburn hair. It was damp.

"Hadley, your hair is wet."

"I went for a swim."

Ernest smiled, arching an eyebrow. "You went swimming before our wedding?"

She nodded.

He was about to place the wreath on her head when she stepped back.

"Wait," she said. "I have something to tell you first: I love you."

"I love you, too."

* * *

His wounded legs made it hard for him to kneel down. With Hadley kneeling beside him, he heard the minister say, "Do you, Elizabeth Hadley Richardson, take this man, Ernest Miller Hemingway, to be your wedded husband in the holy state of matrimony? To love, honor, and keep him, in sickness and in health, for better or for worse, till death do you part?"

Hadley looked at Ernest and nodded decisively.

"I do," she said.

* * *

A short time later Grace Hemingway took her son aside.

"Ernest," she said, choosing her words carefully, "ever since you decided you didn't need any further guidance from me, I've tried to keep silent and let you work out your own salvation. But I shall brave your anger and speak my mind one last time."

Ernest took a breath and waited. She continued.

"Stop your loafing and pleasure seeking, Son. Stop borrowing money without a thought of paying it back. Stop trying to live off anybody and everybody. You have certain obligations now, to your wife—"

"And to God, and our savior Jesus Christ. I know, Mother."

She looked into his eyes for a moment, then smiled and ran her hand across his cheek tenderly. "Take good care of her—and yourself." Then she went to Hadley and hugged her.

Dr. Hemingway stepped up to Ernest, embraced him, and kissed him on both cheeks. "May the Lord watch over us while we're apart, son," he said. There were tears in his eyes.

Ernest looked away. "So long, Father."

* * *

The luggage was loaded into the old Ford when Ernest's friend, Sherwood Anderson, took the married couple aside.

"What are your plans?"

"Off to Italy," said Hemingway.

"What are you going to live on?"

Ernest smiled. "I have a few lire put aside. We'll be fine."

"And then there's my inheritance," said Hadley. "Not much, but enough to make ends meet."

Anderson was wistful. "Paris is the only place for a serious writer. Living is cheap and the Left Bank is flooded with young artists, painters, writers. You could write for the *Toronto Star*, Ernest. A series of European letters . . ."

"Is that an offer?"

"It is," said the journalist. "That would take care of the rent, don't you think?"

Ernest winked at Hadley. "What do you think, Hash?"

She put her arms around her husband and hugged him. "I'd be happy in Paris, as long as you have your writing and I have you."

"I'll take my Corona portable," said Ernest.

Anderson took a pad and pen from his pocket. "I know lots of people there," he said. "You've got to meet Gertrude Stein. She collects modern art. She looks like an Indian and speaks like an angel—strange, wonderful word combinations. I can write you a few letters of introduction and send them on."

"Do it!" shouted Ernest, jumping onto the running board of the Ford. Hadley was already inside.

Waving, they drove off down the road.

Paris—Spring, 1922

Ernest Hemingway, in his worn-out leather jacket and blue sailor sweater, stood before a painting by Paul Cézanne on the wall of Gertrude Stein's long, expansive living room. The provincial landscape was flanked by others by the same artist, as well as several by Matisse and Picasso. Miss Stein approached the young would-be author, and handed him his manuscript.

"Your stories are good, Hemingway," she said. "No question about that. You're a good writer because you write the way you are and you live the way you write."

"Thank you."

"Hold on," she said. "This one here, 'Up in Michigan.' The nocturnal deflowering of the waitress and the lapping waves and the pier. It's *inaccrochable*."

"You mean dirty?"

"Like certain pictures by certain painters which cannot be exhibited in public. They're not bought. You understand, Hemingway?"

He motioned to the wall, covered with paintings.

"How many of those are *inaccrochable*?" he asked.

She laughed. "Do you like paintings?"

"Yes, but I can't afford them. Look at this Cézanne. I'd like to write about landscapes the way he painted them. Look—he's taken the whole thing apart piece by piece and constructed his own reality out of the fragments. No tricks. Something dead serious."

Gertrude Stein looked at the painting as though she were seeing it for the first time.

"Nobody's ever written about a landscape like he painted," said Ernest Hemingway.

"Cézanne didn't just paint what he saw," she said. "He painted truth."

"That's what it's all about! To write a true sentence. Cézanne knew landscapes because they lived inside him. What's going on inside the waitress on the pier . . . that's something *I* know about."

"*Inaccrochable*."

"Why? Because she says it hurts when it happens?"

* * *

In another corner of the room sat Hadley Hemingway and Alice Toklas at a small table. They looked like little children who aren't allowed to talk to the grownups. Hadley surveyed the room.

"Who's that reading aloud over there?" she asked.

"Ezra Pound," said Toklas. "He's a fellow countryman. He writes poetry."

Hadley made a move to get up so she could hear, but Alice Toklas looked at her sternly. "Please remain seated, Mrs. Hemingway."

"But I can't hear him!"

Toklas cut her off. "You'll have to make do with me here. That's the way Miss Stein wants it."

"How very kind of Miss Stein," Hadley replied stiffly.

"Another glass of *eau de vie*?" Alice refilled her glass. Hadley tossed the clear liquid down in one throw.

"Have you been married long, Mrs. Hemingway?"

Vexed, Hadley ignored the question. "Do you actually mean that women are not permitted in her inner circle?" She motioned with her head toward the group of literati, among whom were some women.

"It's the ritual here," said Alice B. Toklas. She tried to change the subject. "Tell me something about yourself, dear. Is it true your husband is nine years younger than you?"

Hadley was not about to be put off. "Who are those women?"

"Unmarried."

"Oh?"

"No wives, Mrs. Hemingway. You understand."

"The ritual. Of course." Fighting boredom, Hadley refilled her glass and tried to get interested in the paintings.

* * *

An hour later, walking unsteadily along the narrow rue de Cardinal Lemoine to their apartment, Hadley told her husband what was on her mind: "Of all the nerve, Ernest. Really, I couldn't care less that they're lesbians, but the way they treated us! Like two well-mannered children whom they forgive for falling in love because they got married."

"Oh, Gertrude's all right," said Hemingway. "Though she does talk a lot of rot sometimes."

Ruffled, Hadley stepped up her pace. "Who am I to say? I'm just your wife!"

"Hadley—"

"Ritual is ritual!"

The owner of the vegetable shop on the corner was taking his products in from the sidewalk because it had started to rain. While Hadley chose some leeks and potatoes, Ernest surveyed the street. From the Bal Musette, a working-class dance hall, came the strains of accordion music. Outside, a few drunks loitered by the entrance. It started raining harder.

Directly across the street from Hemingway, standing in the light of a lantern, was a one-legged street-walker. Looking up and down the street, she ignored the rain. He stared at her, taking everything in.

Hadley emerged from the shop, vegetables gathered to her in her arms. Ernest pulled off his leather jacket and held it over her head while they ran for the door to their building. As he opened the door he turned, looked back up the street. The streetwalker was still standing there. A priest from the nearby Episcopal Church opened his umbrella and held it over her.

* * *

Thunder, lightning, a real storm raging outside. Hadley lay on the large, gold-painted mahogany bed which took up almost the entire one-room apartment. Shivering, she waited for Ernest to undress and slip in beside her.

"Your toes are freezing," he said to her, disappearing under the covers in the direction of her feet. He began rubbing them. His mind was still on the party.

"Gertrude thinks Up in Michigan is *inaccrochable*," he said.

"Why?"

"Because of the sex."

"What does she know about sex?"

"She has her notions."

"Is that all?"

"She considers the male sex act revolting."

"I don't," said Hadley.

"She means between men."

"Oh."

"She says women are different."

"How?"

"They don't do anything revolting."

"What does she mean by revolting?"

"Oh," said her husband, "I don't know. This maybe . . . or maybe this . . . or this . . ."

Hadley stretched, and began to purr.

* * *

"Monsieur Pound is looking for you."

Hemingway looked up from his notebook. Jean, his waiter at the Cafe Closerie des Lilas, placed a *cafe au lait* and two croissants on his table. The small, round, marble tabletop was cluttered with writing materials.

"Where is he?"

"He said to wait for him. He will be here shortly. He says it's very important."

Ernest put his pencil in his pencil sharpener and

turned it slowly, with great care. He pulled a small penknife from his pocket and sharpened the tip. He opened the notebook, smoothed out a page with the ball of his hand, took a small sip of coffee, stared into space for a moment, and began to write.

"I have seen . . . the one-legged streetwalker . . . limping along the pavement . . . through the crowd . . . on a rainy night . . ."

At that moment Ezra Pound, a tall man with red hair in disarray, goatee untrimmed, appeared in the doorway. Spotting Hemingway, he headed for his table.

". . . with a beefy-faced Episcopal clergyman . . . holding an umbrella over her."

Pound took a seat on the bench next to Hemingway. Silently he motioned to Jean for coffee, as though he had no intention of disturbing the young writer. Ernest put a period at the end of his sentence. The tip of his pencil broke off. Visibly pleased with his work, he closed his notebook and looked at Ezra Pound.

"You were looking for me, Ezra?"

Pound nodded, taking a notebook from the inside pocket of his jacket. "Yes," he said wearily. "I'm collecting for *Bel Esprit*."

"Bel Esprit?"

"A fund I've founded. The idea is that we all contribute a portion of whatever we earn."

"What for?"

"It's so that Mr. Eliot will have enough money to get out of the bank."

"Major Eliot?"

"T. S. Eliot. He works in a bank."

"What's a major doing in a bank? He couldn't hack the military anymore?"

"What makes you think he's a major?"

"Isn't he?"

"Of course not!"

"Well, what is he?"

"He's a writer!"

Hemingway sipped his *cafe au lait*, took a bite of croissant. "Seems Mr. Eliot has quite a few jobs, Ezra. Works in a bank, writes, a major in the army. He must be earning pretty well as it is."

Pound held out his empty palm in front of Hemingway's face. "That is just the point, you see. If he has to work he can't write. Well . . . ?"

Hemingway dug into his pocket and pulled out his last few francs. He handed them to the poet, who, satisfied, wrote down the amount of the contribution in his little notebook.

Hemingway slumped in his chair. "Writing's the hardest job there is, Ezra. If your friend doesn't want to work he'd be better off staying in the bank."

"Thank you, Ernest. Either you have *esprit,* or you don't. By the way, I sent six of your poems to Scofield Thayer."

Stunned, Ernest looked at Ezra. "You did?"

"They'll be published in *Dial.* And, pending approval, you'll have a story for the *Little Review.*"

Hemingway smiled. "Ezra, you're a true friend. And a wonderful editor. You're going to teach me how to write!"

Flattered, Pound returned the smile. "But only if you'll teach me how to box!"

Playfully, Ernest punched his friend on the shoulder. "Now, there's a real pal!" he said. "As though sticking your neck out for me weren't enough. Now you're going to let me caress your cheeks with the big gloves!"

* * *

Spring, wetter than usual, was still with Paris as Hemingway entered *Shakespeare and Company,* a small bookstore and lending library at 12 rue de l'Odéon. Browsing before the shelves packed with books, he chose several and handed them to Sylvia Beach, the American proprietress, who considered herself a friend to all writers, especially those writing in English.

"I'll take *A Sportsman's Sketches* by Turgenev. And *Sons and Lovers*," he said.

A small, neat woman, she smiled pleasantly. "You may take more if you want."

"Fine. I'll take the Garnett edition of *War and Peace* and *The Gambler and Other Stories* by Dostoyevsky."

"You won't be back for ages if you read all that, Ernest."

"I'll be back to pay."

She blushed, placed her hands together carefully. "I didn't mean it that way. You pay whenever it's convenient." She stamped the books and registered them in a catalog. "Just don't read too fast."

"I won't."

"Oh," she said, taking a letter from the small counter, "I almost forgot your mail. A letter from Toronto."

Hemingway opened the letter, read it, and smiled at Sylvia Beach. "Sherwood Anderson. The *Toronto Star* wants me to go to Italy!"

"How nice."

"They want me to interview Mussolini and write about his Fascist movement. Ever been to Italy?"

She shook her head. "No, but I know it's supposed to be very beautiful there."

"The first time I went there I knew nothing about the country, the people, the . . ."

"When was that?"

"It was during the war."

Venice—Spring, 1922

Hadley stood at the window of the Casa Frolo, a modest hotel with a marvelous view of the Santa Maria della Salute from Plaza Saint Marco. Daylight streamed into the room as Ernest, sitting on the large double bed, pulled on his boots.

"It was so strange, Hash," he said, his voice flat, eyes staring into the distance. "The shrapnel didn't even hurt at first. Just felt like my boots were full of warm water. But then the machine gun opened up. I got it in the knee, this one. Knocked me flat. I could hardly get back up. My jacket was soaked with the Italian's blood and my pants looked like someone had made black-currant jelly in them and then drilled some holes to squeeze it out. Wasn't a very pretty sight . . ."

They spent the morning touring the canals by gondola, the afternoon on foot, a slow crawl from bar to bar. Hemingway was preoccupied, his mind reverting to the awful experiences of war. They turned in early, and sleep came, but did not last. In the absolute darkness of early morning Ernest sat upright in bed, grasping his leg.

"Oh God, help me! Help me!" he cried.

Hadley woke instantly, putting her arms around his broad shoulders and hugging him. "Ernest! Wake up!"

His eyes opened, he exhaled.

"You were dreaming, Ernest."

"Oh, Hadley, I'd forgotten. I'd blocked it all out . . ."

"Tell me."

"When you're eighteen and you go off to war, you have all these big illusions . . . about your immortality. The others might get wounded, or killed, but not you. Because you're invincible. You're invincible *because* you're you, and because you're young. But then, once you've been badly wounded . . . it changes all that."

She kissed him tenderly. When he relaxed, she stood, draped a bathrobe over her shoulders, and went to the window.

"Tatie? I want a melon," she said.

"You want a melon?"

"I've got this craving for a melon. Could you get me one?"

"It's four o'clock in the morning, Hash."

"I want it to be daylight." She went to the mirror. "I want to let my hair grow again."

"That's nice, Hash."

"I don't want to run around like a tomboy anymore. And I want it to be a girl. Or a boy. I want . . ."

He stared at her, his eyes widening. "Does that mean . . ."

"Mean what?"

"You're pregnant?"

She nodded.

"How long have you known?"

"Since Milan."

"Milan!"

"Milan."

"We weren't careful enough."

"What do you mean? Aren't you happy?" She sat beside him on the bed, but they did not touch until he took her hand.

"Of course I'm happy."

She turned to him accusingly. "Come on. You're scared. Admit it."

"Admit what?"

"You're scared the baby might muscle in on your mobility."

"Hey, what about you?"

Hadley smiled, She was radiant, beaming. "I think it's wonderful! And I want it to be born in America. And then I want all three of us to come back to Paris. But I want a nicer apartment. I want a cat . . ."

He put his arms around her and squeezed. "You'll have it all, Hash."

"What do you want?"

"*You*, featherpuss."

Paris—Spring, 1924

It was 7:00 A.M. Ernest Hemingway flung open the door to his apartment building on the rue Notre Dame des Champs and found his favorite goatherd milking a goat into an earthen jug. He felt good. He paid the goatherd, took the jug, and disappeared into the house.

Hadley came into the kitchen and found her husband bouncing their son, John Hadley Nicanor, alias "Bumby," at the table. By his feet their fat, brown-striped cat licked goat's milk from a saucer.

"Dix bis avenue des Gobelins," sang Hemingway as he spooned porridge into the infant, *"Dix bis avenue des Gobelins . . ."*

Hadley leaned against the doorway, smiling. Her hair was longer and she had gained weight, but she was more beautiful than ever.

> *"Dix bis avenue des Gobelins,*
> *Dix bis avenue des Gobelins,*
> *Dix bis avenue des Gobelins,*
> That's where my Bumby lives!"

Ernest gave the baby an extra bounce. "Come on, Bumby, sing along!"

Hadley laughed. "He can't even talk yet."

"He could at least sing along! After all, in the course of his prenatal life he spent six months on skis, attended five bullfights, and crossed the Atlantic Ocean! Come on, kid, sing along with Papa. *Dix bis avenue des Gobelins . . ."*

Hadley joined them at the table. "What are you teaching him anyway?"

"His baby-sitter's address. Say we're off on a trip and he gets lost here in Paris. All he has to do is start singing and people will know where to bring him." Ernest handed the baby to Hadley and picked up the cat. "And how are you, Mr. Featherpuss?"

Suddenly a shadow seemed to pass over Hadley's face. She hugged the baby, then looked at her husband. "Trip? Ernest, I have to shop all over Paris to find the best food bargains. My shoes have holes in them, my clothes—we won't even talk about my clothes. And you talk about going off on another trip."

"I just meant suppose we got some extra money—"

"*Money?* We haven't had any money coming in since you stopped writing for the *Star.*"

Hemingway eyed his wife, spoke evenly. "We haven't any money because your friend George Breaker lost everything we had speculating on the stock market."

"It was *my* money he lost."

"Okay, your money."

"He meant well."

"Sure. Selling $19,000 worth of United Railway for $10,000!"

"It wasn't his fault!" shouted Hadley.

Furious, Ernest stormed out into the hallway and put on his beret. Carrying the baby, Hadley followed him.

"Where are you going?"

"To make some money!"

The door slammed.

* * *

He wore black gym shorts and boxing gloves. Warming up in a corner of the big, musty gym in the rue Pointoise, Ernest shadowboxed, skipped rope, and worked with the heavy bag. At the far end of the room was a raised boxing ring, where a professional heavyweight fought his sparring partner in the presence of a trainer. Hemingway eyed the ring from time to time, hoping for a chance. He got it.

In the ring the professional flattened his partner with a lightning right. The man picked himself up, shook his head, and pulled off his gloves.

"But, Henri," pleaded the trainer.

"I've had it, Jacques! No more for today. Find somebody else."

The trainer looked around for a suitable substitute, spotted Hemingway. "Hey, Hem! Up to a few rounds?"

Ernest was skipping rope. "How much?"

"Ten francs a round."

Harold Loeb, boxing fan and literary success, went over to Ernest. "Careful, Hem," he said. "He has a nasty right."

"He has the trickiest right in the business, Harold."

"What's so tricky about it?"

"He uses his *left!* Har har har!" Hemingway stepped into the ring.

The professional and Ernest boxed seriously and elegantly while Loeb and the trainer looked on. The pro was considerably quicker, but Hemingway knew how to deflect, weaken, or absorb the blows. The bout grew rougher. Ernest hit back a little too hard on several occasions. The professional moved in, driving him around the ring.

"I think perhaps you'd better stop them," said Loeb.

The trainer hit the bell. "Time!"

The pro gave Hemingway a playful smack with his open glove before heading to his corner. Ernest was furious. Unable to suppress a momentary burst of rage, he clipped the pro on the back of his head. Amazed, the pro spun around. The two men stared at each other momentarily. Then, just as the heavyweight was about to throw himself on Ernest, the trainer grabbed him from behind and pulled him away.

Ernest acknowledged his mistake with a shrug as he climbed from the ring. The trainer paid him his ten francs.

"I thought a writer would have more brains,

Hem," he said. "A good sparring partner can keep his temper. You can't."

"I was afraid he was going to knock your block off, old man," said Harold Loeb. "Why take chances like that?"

"I need the money," said Hemingway, still seething.

"Money? I'd be happy to lend you some," said Loeb.

A sneer appeared on Ernest's face. "I don't need your money."

Embarrassed, Loeb steered the conversation to another subject. "By the way, Leon Fleischman is in Pars. He's Liveright's literary agent."

"Never heard of him." Ernest pulled off his gloves.

"He's brought the contract for *Doodab*."

"*Doodab?*" Disgusted, Hemingway spat out the word.

"Didn't I tell you? Liveright's publishing my new novel."

"Wonderful."

"Say, why don't I introduce you? Maybe he'll like your stuff."

Ernest took a deep breath, managed to suppress his jealous anger. He said nothing.

Harold Loeb was enthusiastic. "Listen, Hem. Let's celebrate tonight. We'll go to the Nègre de Toulouse. Bring Hadley. My treat."

* * *

The famous restaurant was completely packed. M. Lavigne, the owner, was making his nightly rounds when he came across Ernest, Hadley, Harold, and two young American women sitting at a large round table. One of the women, Kitty Cannell, was blond with blue eyes and very pale skin. The other, Pauline Pfeiffer, mid twenties, was short with a wide, silver headband around her black, bobbed hair. In her elegant white evening gown she looked as if she'd just stepped from the pages of a fashion magazine. Lavigne eyed her for an extra moment, then greeted Ernest and Hadley as old acquaintances.

"Ah, Monsieur, Madame Hemingway! Monsieur, ladies . . . welcome, welcome all!" Then he looked at Hemingway.

"You know, I saw monsieur recently in the Closerie des Lilas, but you were so busy . . ."

"That's my office, where I work," said Ernest, grinning.

"And your work? Is it progressing well?"

"It's going pretty well. Little by little."

"And your fascinating friends?"

"Yes, my friends. This is Harold Loeb, Princeton man and editor of the excellent art magazine *Broom*. And this enchanting woman here is Kitty Cannell from Ithaca. She's Paris's next prima ballerina. And yes, as you've correctly assumed, Monsieur Lavigne, they are a couple in love."

Harold and Kitty looked at each other and laughed nervously. Hemingway motioned to Pauline, leaned toward her, and gave her his most charming smile.

"And this is Pauline Pfeiffer. A journalist."

He leaned over to Harold, whispered, "She any good?"

"Writes about clothes."

Ernest glanced back at the proprietor. "As you've doubtless noticed, Monsieur Lavigne, Miss Pfeiffer is offering us a glimpse of the latest range in haute couture."

Monsieur Lavigne bowed deeply. Ernest turned toward Harold.

"And since this kind gentleman is treating us," he

said with a wink to everyone at the table, "we'll have
. . . lobster! Lobster from Brittany, of course. And
some Pouilly Fuissé 1917!"

"*Ah bon!* One minute!" Making a clicking sound
with his tongue, M. Lavigne hurried to the kitchen.
Ernest turned back to Pauline.

"And what exactly does one write about clothes,
Miss Pfeiffer?" he inquired politely.

She was serious. "I cover the latest fashions in
Paris, Mr. Hemingway. That's primarily what my readers are interested in."

Ernest raised an eyebrow. "Your readers? And, of
course, years of journalistic training have preceded
your reputation?"

Hadley and Kitty looked at Ernest in disbelief.
Hadley was embarrassed, Kitty amused. Pauline was at
first taken aback by the rudeness, but Hemingway's
smile told her something else.

"Naturally, Mr. Hemingway," she said. "More
than a few." She got up from the table, going in the
direction of the powder room. Hadley and Kitty rose
and followed her.

Pauline was touching up her face as Hadley and
Kitty entered.

"You mustn't take him seriously," said Hadley.

Pauline smiled, touched Hadley's shoulder.
"Thanks for the inside information." She left.

Kitty was at the mirror, elegant, pink, white, and
gold, with the pronounced good posture of a ballerina.
Joining her, Hadley regarded her own image, noting the
difference. By comparison, her appearance was definitely matronly. Kitty powdered her nose and cheeks,
checked her makeup, lipstick. Hadley watched her, full
of admiration. She took Kitty's little golden perfume
bottle, sniffed. Kitty nodded assent and Hadley gave
herself a quick spray.

"How long have you known Pauline?" she asked.

"Oh, she knows people who know Harold. She

just sort of tagged along. Rich. Really loaded. Her family owns half of Arkansas. Princess Pauline of Piggott, ha! If you ask me, she's here to find a good match."

"She's so . . . so different."

"Heck. She has all her stuff done by Coco Chanel. Expensive as hell."

Hadley lowered her eyes, a trace of sadness to her expression. Kitty shook her head. She took off her earrings and put them on Hadley's ears.

"Can I ask you something sort of personal?"

Hadley looked at her, waiting.

"How do you hack it?" Kitty asked. "The way he makes you live . . . I mean, why did he give up journalism? Throws away his job and then has a baby. I don't get it."

Hadley shrugged. "He said it was either journalism or writing. They're not the same and you can't do both. He decided he wanted to write. That's what he wants to do. And he's good."

"You sure must be stuck on him."

Hadley was about to take off the earrings, but Kitty stopped her. "No, no. Keep them. They look much better on you anyway."

Hadley hugged her friend. "You know, Ernest and I love each other. We eat well, drink good wine, sometimes we go to the racetrack, and in the winter we're taking Bumby to the mountains. We get by—truly—and one day Ernest is going to be a great writer."

"And what about you?" asked Kitty Cannell.

When Kitty and Hadley returned to the table they were barely noticed.

"Ford Maddox Ford is a great novelist," Hemingway explained to his avid listeners. "At least, that's what he'll tell you every chance he gets. But I question his expertise as a publisher. His choice of writers—"

"Evidently he considers T. S. Eliot the living Christ among poets," interjected Harold Loeb.

Ernest laughed heartily. "Exactly. Oh yes, it seems Ezra has rescued Eliot from the bank!"

"Good old Ezra," Hadley chimed in. "Ranting and raving and doing his best to spur the Rive Gauche on to meaningful literary activity."

Harold Loeb grew serious. "If Ezra Pound would focus all that time and energy on his own writing instead of on others', he could be a truly fine poet again."

Ernest looked at Harold. In a moment his good mood vanished.

"Ezra Pound helps poets," he said. "He helps painters, sculptors, and writers whom he believes in. He defends them when they're attacked. He gets them into magazines. He gets them out of prison. He lends them money, he talks them out of suicide. He's my friend, Harold."

"I'm sure he is," said Loeb, wondering what was coming.

"He'd even help *you*," said Ernest, scowling. "If you ever needed his help. But thank God you don't. Isn't that right, Harold?"

"Take it easy," said Loeb, trying to soften the situation. "I didn't mean it that way. I've nothing, absolutely nothing, against Ezra Pound."

The lobsters, fresh and kicking, arrived with the wine. Ernest stood and examined the crustations carefully. He turned one over and discovered a mound of small red eggs.

"The meat of the female lobster," he intoned, "is tastier and more tender while they're carrying eggs. This gal's pretty heavy for her size. Let's see, we'll have this one, that one, that and that . . . and we'll have them *à la thermidore,* of course."

At that moment Leon Fleischman, one of New York's most successful literary agents, arrived and was introduced. He took a seat next to Harold Loeb, and clapped him on the back.

"Congratulations, Loeb," he said. "Liveright has decided to print five thousand copies of your novel, and that's just for starters. The book is going to be a huge success!"

Harold Loeb beamed. Fleischman turned to Hemingway.

"I read one of your stories not too long ago, Hemingway," he said. "'My Old Man.' A good racetrack story. Sherwood Anderson couldn't have written it better himself."

Hemingway took a sip from his glass. "No, I doubt it," he said evenly. "My story is about a young boy and his father, and about horse racing. Sherwood has also written about boys and horse racing, but my story was influenced by boys and horses."

There was an awkward silence. Leon Fleischman got up. "I'd be pleased if you would send me a few of your stories, Hemingway," he said. "If I like them I'll recommend them to Liveright." He bowed and left the table. Loeb went with him to the bar, where they talked privately. He returned.

At the table, Ernest discovered Hadley's new earrings. "Where did you get those?" he demanded.

"Kitty gave them to me," said Hadley. "Aren't they lovely?"

Hemingway brought his open hand down upon the table. "A gift from Harold? How very generous, Harold. Give them back, Hadley. Give them back to her!"

Hadley shook her head in disgust. "Oh, you're in rare form tonight," she said.

"Top form," said Ernest, glaring.

Hadley removed the earrings and handed them to Kitty. She got up and ran out of the restaurant. Ernest followed her.

"He hates women," said Kitty to Harold Loeb. "Jesus, did you see the look he gave me?"

"He's . . . under some strain," said Loeb.

Kitty squeezed his arm. "You better watch it,

Harold," she said. "Or one day he'll kick you right in the teeth."

* * *

Hadley was running up the stairway to their apartment when Ernest caught her. She was crying. He put his arms around her.

"Forgive me, Hash," he pleaded. "I tried. But all day long I was so furious with him."

"Why? What did he do?" she sobbed.

"Nothing. It's just that feeling you get when you know you're better, but the other guy's getting the breaks."

There was a pause. Hadley nodded, patted her husband's broad back. "I guess that hurts," she said, understandingly.

"They'll see," he said, holding her tightly. "I'll show the bastards."

She laid her hand on his arm soothingly. "I know, Tatie."

Switzerland—Winter, 1924/1925

Ernest sat at a small table near a window. Outside, the sun was rising over the snow-covered peaks of the Swiss Alps. The hotel room was warm and cozy, a good place to write. Even so, he wore a thick scarf around his neck, a long sweater pulled over his pajamas, the arms pulled down as far as possible, so that only the tips of his fingers were visible.

Carefully, one sentence at a time, he wrote in his little blue notebook. Now and then he would steal a glance at Hadley, who was almost completely buried under a big goose-down quilt.

"Want to hear?"

Hadley nodded, stretching like a cat.

Hemingway began to read aloud the scene he had just written. In it he portrayed a young American woman in a hotel room. He described the scene economically—catching her mood and the room in a few short sentences.

The woman had boyishly short hair, which she tells her companion she is tired of. She goes on to elaborate on the other things she would like to make her happy.

As he read, Hadley started to smile, for she perceived the similarity between the woman in the story's words and similar feelings she had recently expressed to Ernest.

Ernest stopped. He looked at Hadley, who laughed.

"And I want a melon," she said. "And you're stealing *our* stories, you crook!"

"Only the good ones."

* * *

Hadley and Bumby were lying warmly wrapped up on chaises longues on the hotel veranda when they heard a shout.

"Hadley! Look, you won't believe it!" Ernest was running up the snow-covered street from the town, waving an opened letter. He sprang to the terrace, caught his breath. His hands were shaking.

"Read! Read the letter! I'm going to have a book published! *In Our Time!*"

Hadley squealed. Bumby waved his fat fists at his father.

"Boni and Liveright are going to publish *In Our Time!* Listen: 'Your splendid collection of stories . . . would like to offer you a contract . . . advance of two hundred dollars.'"

He hugged her, still clutching the letter. "I made it, Hash. This is the big breakthrough. I knew it. I'm going to win. I'm going to be praised by the highbrows and read by the lowbrows!"

He took his wife's hand. "Come on," he said, pulling her to her feet.

"What, where?"

"We'll light a candle."

* * *

Hand in hand they walked to the little village church. Hadley paused, looked at Ernest objectively.

"You know the first thing I noticed about you? The thing that attracted me to you?"

Ernest shrugged.

"The way you walk. So big, and paddy, and rhythmic. You still walk that way, and I still love it."

"You mean all I have to do is walk and you'll like me?"

Hadley made a snowball and threw it at him. He dived for her, catching her around the waist and pulling her down. She looked at him, big, burly and tanned from the skiing that had occupied them for weeks.

"What did you like about me the first time you saw me?" she asked.

"Your red hair," he replied, stroking it. "It was still wet when we walked into the church. You took a dip before our wedding!"

They arrived at the small chapel. Ernest opened the door with a large, glittering silver key. He winked at her.

"How many nicknames can I still remember? Let's see: Hemingstein, Nesto, Hemmy, Oinbones . . . where'd *Oinbones* come from?"

"I don't know," he said, growing serious. "It seems like such a long time ago. I guess it was just a noise, kid's stuff. I forget."

"Me too."

"But I'll never forget anything we've done, anything we've said. I'll remember everything!"

They entered the church. The small interior was covered with frescoes. In a corner was a small candle-stand with many candles. Ernest dropped a few coins in the offertory box, selected a candle, and lit it. For a moment he stood there, then turned around. Putting his arm around Hadley's shoulders, he walked her out through an arched portal to the village cemetery. In front of them was a magnificent Alpine panorama. He lifted her chin and looked deeply into her eyes.

"This will always be our place, Hadley. One of our special places."

She nodded.

"I love you so."

"And I love you," she replied.

He waved an arm at the mountains. "You know, the right time to die is when you're happy. When you're going flat out, not hesitating, afraid of nothing. Just being and knowing you're doing it right . . . I hope when it comes I'll die like that."

Hadley started to cry softly. She put a finger to his lips. "Don't . . . stop . . . you mustn't talk that way."

He wiped her tears away. "Hey, come on. You're not scared? I was just thinking about being happy. Aren't you happy?"

Paris—Summer, 1925

Hadley sat sipping ice tea with Kitty at a white table in front of the clubhouse. Close by on the tennis court Ernest and Harold were fighting their way through a vicious volley. Harold Loeb, as usual, had the upper hand.

"Sometimes I think Ernest would like to knock the balls right through him," said Kitty, shaking her head.

"He can't stand losing," Hadley observed.

"No kidding."

Ernest had worked his way forward from the base-
line to the net, but then he hit the ball out of bounds.

"Forty all!" shouted Pauline from her perch on the
umpire's chair. Harold fetched the ball and served.

"Look at her," Kitty said, nodding toward
Pauline. "You think she ever lets up? The hair, the
pearls, the makeup, the whole perfect round-the-clock
chic. Think she ever slips? Maybe when it's dark and
no one's around to see?"

"She is pretty," Hadley conceded.

"Okay, but she never steps out of the bandbox!"

"I guess it just goes with the job," Hadley said.
"If you work in Paris for *Vogue* magazine . . ."

"She's not at work now. She's playing hookey . . .
playing something. Do you think this is her idea of
slumming? Do you go slumming in full war paint?"

Hadley laughed, bounced Bumby on her knee.
"What is this, anyway? I thought Pauline was a friend
of yours. She's a nice, generous girl. and besides, who
am I going to have when you're gone? Pauline'll keep
me on my toes. I can't be a drudge around her." Hadley
sat up, took off her sunglasses.

"What about you and Harold? Is everything really
all over?"

Kitty shrugged. "I don't know what went wrong.
We'll stay good friends . . ."

At that moment a large green convertible pulled
up in front of the clubhouse. From it stepped a slim
woman, thirtyish, wearing a very masculine tweed suit
and a man's felt hat on her short blond hair. She leaned
nonchalantly against the car, watching the tennis
match. Hadley looked from her to Kitty, and back
again.

"Is that what went wrong?"

Kitty nodded, adjusting her sunglasses. "That's
Lady Duff Twysden. The man in the car is Pat Guthrie,
a Scottish drunk she's living with till her divorce comes

through. Half the men in Montparnasse think they're in love with her."

"She's beautiful. Her face is as thin and delicate as a cameo."

"A nymphomaniac. If you ask me, she's probably frigid. Hangs out with Pat's friends—all homosexuals. She never wears makeup. Word is she never washes. A real lush. She drinks men under the table. And Harold is simply nuts about her."

Hadley touched Kitty's hand. She sensed her trying to downplay her feelings.

"We never wanted to get married anyway."

* * *

Ernest and Harold finished their tennis game and, as usual, Harold won. Furious, Ernest flung his racket to the ground, suppressing a curse. Breathing deeply, he took a moment to compose himself, control his emotions. He went to Harold and congratulated him. Watching the two men, Pauline came down from the umpire's chair and sat with Hadley and Kitty.

"I have to laugh," said Pauline to no one in particular.

"Yes?" Hadley asked.

"Ernest is certainly not a very gracious loser."

"But he sure as hell loves to win," said Kitty.

* * *

A little later, when Ernest and Harold had changed their clothes, they spoke for a moment with Lady Duff. In a good mood now, Ernest rubbed his hands together and shouted to the women so that everyone could hear, "Well, what do you say? I feel like getting drunk tonight. Do any of you need an invitation?"

Lady Duff opened the door to the convertible. Harold got in the back and she followed. Without a word Pat Guthrie handed Harold a silver flask.

Cradling Bumby, Hadley went to her husband. "I want to get Bumby home. You go on without me."

Ernest gave her a cursory kiss good-bye and got in the backseat with Harold and Duff.

"I won't be back late," he shouted, "or sober!"

Hadley watched the car drive off, then returned to the table. "Sometimes he just has to blow off a little steam," she said, feeling the need to explain. "He's still young."

"You're not," said Kitty.

Hadley stiffened. After a moment Kitty added in a gentler tone, "Sorry. I'm just trying to be a friend."

Hadley ran her hand through Bumby's hair, shook her head. "We're fine, Kitty," she said. "Really we are."

* * *

At the American Bar at the Closerie des Lilas it was still daylight when Ernest, Harold, Duff, and her escort, Pat, sat together at the bar. Pat Guthrie tried in vain to build a Chinese tower out of the cardboard beer coasters—tried and tried again. Ernest was waxing eloquent, talking loudly, somewhat drunkenly, about bullfighting, his favorite subject that spring. From time to time Harold whispered something to Duff, running his lips over her ear. The bottle in front of Ernest was almost empty.

"Harold," he said, pounding the bar, "you mean you've never been to a bullfight? It's something you've got to experience! You're coming with us to Spain this summer and the hell with everything else."

Ernest took another drink. His voice grew louder.

"Fiesta in Pamplona! God, they have bullfights in that town. The most beautiful confrontation with death you'll ever see. Every corrida is a great tragedy. It takes guts and skill and more guts."

With that, Ernest jumped to his feet. He took off

his coat and demonstrated a few veronicas, then went back to the bar.

"It beats boxing and tennis and horse racing and—"

"Sex?" Duff asked.

Hemingway looked at her, laughed, shouted to the waiter for another bottle.

"Aren't you drinking just a little too fast, Hem?" asked Harold Loeb.

Ernest held up his hands. "*Everyone* drinks too fast in Paris. That's the fashion. Difference is, I like getting drunk. The only remorse I ever feel is the gastric kind. Next day I work it off." He raised his glass to Duff, who reciprocated.

"Now, here's a girl who shows a lot of promise," he said.

Lady Duff tried not to laugh.

* * *

It was raining hard and the Paris streets were deserted. Completely soaked, Ernest climbed the stairway to the apartment, leaving a trail of water in his wake. He unlocked the door and stepped inside.

"Hadley?"

Pauline Pfeiffer lay sound asleep on the couch, a book in her hands. Ernest stumbled into a table, waking her.

"What are you doing here?" he asked, his eyes slightly out of focus.

"I'm just looking after Bumby," she explained. "Hadley asked me to."

"Where's Hadley?"

"She was worried and went out to look for you."

Ernest dropped his wet things on the floor and went to the bedroom. Pauline picked everything up and took it to the kitchen to dry. When she returned, the door to the bedroom was open and Ernest was standing by the bed changing. For a moment Pauline watched him. He turned and caught her in the act. Embarrassed, she looked away.

"Never seen a man getting changed?" he asked.

Pauline sat at the table and pretended to read.

"I spoke with somebody about you yesterday," she said.

Ernest turned around. "Oh yeah? What'd they say?"

Pauline was about to reply when she saw Hadley standing in the doorway. She too was soaking wet. Ernest looked at her, slightly amazed.

"Where've you been?" he asked, slurring his words.

Hadley gestured vaguely toward the street. "I felt like getting drunk tonight, like you. I looked all over for you. Hi, Pauline."

"You've been drinking," said Ernest gravely.

"So have you."

"Yeah, but I can hold mine."

Hadley was swaying. She sat down. "I'm just trying to keep up."

Ernest went to her, kneeled beside her. "Hadley, what's wrong with you?"

She shook her head sadly. "If I don't keep up, I'll lose you. I don't want to lose you, so I drink."

"What kind of nonsense is that?" Ernest asked.

The situation was getting more and more uncomfortable for Pauline. She got up, went to the kitchen. "I'll make some strong coffee for the two of you," she said.

She put on some water, found the last coffee beans, and put them into the grinder. Before she ground them she listened to what was going on in the living room. Ernest was holding Hadley, rocking her back and forth. He spoke into her ear, rhythmically, softly, but Pauline could hear the words.

"What a bunch of silly thoughts, Hash. Nobody's

losing anyone here. We'll go to Spain! Fiesta in Pamplona. Remember? The rough, wild countryside. The Pyrenees. The huge beech forests that have never seen an ax, and the ice-cold streams full of trout. The only country in Europe that hasn't been shot to hell. And the bullfights! Do you remember? The tragedy entitled 'death of the bull.' The most beautiful thing we ever saw together. Like having a ringside seat in a war where nothing can happen to you."

Pauline came into the room carrying the coffeepot and two mugs. Ernest looked at her.

"Hey, want to come with us to Spain?"

She dropped her eyes, shook her head.

"No, I'm going to Italy," she said.

Pamplona—Summer, 1925

The square was deserted, the hot midday sun bearing down. White wicker chairs were set up under the shady arcades. The cafes around the square were almost empty. The waiters were standing around, bored, chasing away the flies with their white napkins. A few young dogs were barking in front of the hotel driveway. The proprietor was dozing in a rocking chair.

Suddenly the old blue-and-yellow post bus arrived, and the whole square roared to life. Visitors there for the festival streamed out of the bus, all carrying wicker hampers filled with food and drink. Laughing loudly, Ernest and Hadley, Duff, Harold, and Pat Guthrie said good-bye to their fellow passengers. The proprietor hurried over.

"Welcome, welcome, Senor Ernesto! Senora! You have the same rooms as last year. Everything is ready."

Hemingway took him aside. "Any news about the bulls?"

"They are bringing in the Vilar bulls this evening

and tomorrow the Miuras. Are you going to the *Desencajonada?*"

Ernest looked to see if Hadley was listening. She wasn't. He nodded.

"And your friends, senor. Are they aficionados?"

Ernest nodded. "One of them came all the way from Scotland to see the fights at San Fermin."

"Oh? But not as aficionado as you."

"They will be once they've seen the fights."

"Hey, Hem!" shouted Duff. "What I need is a warm bed!"

"A cold drink would be more to my liking," said Pat Guthrie.

* * *

That evening they all had drinks in the comfortable wicker chairs of the arcade. It was a quiet night and Ernest's soft, low voice could be heard clearly by all.

"Come nightfall, the bulls are unloaded and transferred from their cages to the corrals where the steers are," he said, almost whispering.

"And what do the steers do?" Duff wanted to know.

"First they run around like scared rabbits. Then they go over to the bulls and try to make friends. They give them a sniff, try to calm them down. Like this."

Ernest's head was very close to Duff's. He sniffed at her neck, at her ear. Harold looked over at Hadley, who looked away. Duff threw back her head and let out her deep, throaty laugh.

"Sometimes the bulls turn on the steers and slash them up," Ernest continued, filling his glass with wine. "They use their horns like a boxer uses his fists! They'll throw a straight left, then an uppercut with the right."

Harold edged his chair somewhat closer to Duff's. "A real dog's life, being a steer," he joked.

Pat was drinking fast and hard. His eyes blurred,

he looked at Harold venomously. "What have you got against it?" he asked with a sneer.

"How do you mean?"

"They have a peaceful life, steers," said Pat. "They just loaf around. They don't have to bother with the opposite sex. Why, it would be ideal for you."

Duff looked at Pat warningly. "Stop it, Pat. You're drunk," she said.

"I am not drunk. I mean it. Would Harold Loeb chase around after Lady Duff if he were a steer?" Guthrie leaned forward. Suddenly he was completely sober. "Have you slept with her? Speak up, Harold! Of course, she's slept with lots of different chaps. But really: have you ever considered the way I might feel?"

Duff looked angrily at Pat. "Would you be quiet!" she admonished.

But Pat went on. "Duff has a large repertoire of amorous tales. She tells me everything."

Duff turned to Ernest. "He always carries on this way when he's drunk," she said weakly. "It's best to just ignore him."

Ernest acted as though nothing had happened. He spoke in the same soft, even tone. "The night before the *Encierro,* the bulls are brought into a pen."

"And then?" Duff asked, leaning closer.

"Then, the next morning, at exactly six o'clock, they shoot off a rocket and the fiesta begins."

Hadley yawned, looked at the stars.

*   *   *

The next morning at exactly six o'clock Duff and Hadley stood on their hotel room balcony looking down at the empty street. All of the adjacent balconies were packed with expectant spectators. Suddenly a rocket blazed into the sky and exploded. There was a cheer, then silence, as everyone looked down the street, waiting for the bulls.

Duff turned around, looked into the room where

Pat Guthrie, still fully dressed, lay on the bed. Beside him was a bottle of Scotch, from which he took a long pull.

Duff shook her head. "Why aren't you down there with Ernest and Harold, you idle lounge lizard?"

"I might spill my drink," he answered.

"Coward!"

In the distance, cries from the crowd could be heard. They grew louder.

"I just hope nothing happens to him," said Hadley. "Every year people get killed. And there are always a few who get gored or trampled."

Duff looked over at Hadley, a slightly mocking expression on her face. Hadley noticed. She shook her head stubbornly.

"I'm sorry. I can't help worrying about Ernest."

Duff motioned to the street below, where the first bunch of people were just running by.

"I wouldn't worry about what's going on down there," she said ominously.

There was something triumphant in Duff's voice. For a moment Hadley looked at her, visibly irritated. Duff looked down at the street, where another batch of men ran by, faster than the first. They were running for their lives. Then Ernest and Harold appeared, running hard. Catching sight of Hadley and Duff, Ernest leaped, punched his fist into the air, and vaulted over a fence. Harold Loeb was already there, waiting for him. A bull flew by, his horns inches from Hemingway's shoulders.

"That was close," said Harold hoarsely.

"They're damn fast. They can do a hundred yards in seven seconds."

"I'm winded."

"Do you like it?"

"Of course I like it! We must absolutely do it again."

"Again? We'll do it every morning, the whole week!"

"I'm with you," said Harold.

* * *

That afternoon when lunch was over, Ernest and Duff, the last to leave, sat at the large round table in the dining room. Most of the other tables had already been cleared and a single waiter hung around the door to the kitchen, gazing lazily about the room. Ernest refilled their glasses with wine. Duff placed her hand on his.

"It makes me feel rather good," she said quietly. "Deciding to do the right thing. And not be a tramp."

Ernest said nothing. She slowly withdrew her hand.

"Hell, I've wanted you, though," she said. "But we can't do it, can we? We can't hurt people. It's what we believe in . . . in place of God, I think. Of course, we all hurt people. It's just that some are different. Hadley. We can't hurt Hadley."

She looked squarely into Ernest's eyes.

"So you mustn't ask me. And I won't ask you. But sometimes when I look at you . . . and I see the way you look at me . . . I don't think I can *stand* it."

At that moment the proprietor rushed in. "Senor, come! You can meet Cayetano Ordoñez!"

Hemingway recognized the famous matador's name instantly. "Great!" he exclaimed. "Where is he?"

"Room 8. He is dressing for the fight. You can come and watch!"

Hemingway nodded toward Duff. "And the lady? Can she come, too?"

Permission was granted.

* * *

There were two beds in Room 8, separated by a partition. An electric light was on, the shutters closed against the merciless midday sun. In a corner was a small altar, a few candles burning in front of a votive picture. Ordoñez, a young man about nineteen years old, stood in the middle of the room. He was wearing a white linen shirt. An adjutant knelt in front of him, fastening a sash around his waist.

The hotel proprietor bowed respectfully, gesturing toward Ernest and Duff, who stood just inside the doorway. "These are passionate aficionados who would like to wish you luck," he said, his voice cracking.

Ordoñez smiled, nodding to them. "You are going to the bullfight?"

Ernest was surprised. "You speak English?"

"I learned English in Gibraltar," the young man explained. "I was born in Ronda. It is very close. Have you seen me in the arena before?"

"Yes, in Madrid."

"The first time, or the second?"

"The first time."

"I was bad then," said Ordoñez with a shrug. "The second time I was better. I am pleased that you like my work. You have not yet seen everything. I will show you something today if I get a good bull."

Duff, who had remained in the background, took a step forward. Ordoñez noticed for the first time—probably because her hair was so short—that she was a woman. He was surprised.

"You want to ask me something?" he inquired politely.

"Do you hate the bulls?"

"Ha! The bulls are my best friends."

"Why kill your best friends?"

"Otherwise they would do it to me," he answered. Turning abruptly to the little altar, he kneeled, genuflected, bowed his head.

* * *

"A fine young man," said the proprietor on their way to the elevator.

"Looks promising," said Hemingway.

"He looks good," said Duff.

Ernest nodded, preoccupied. "Let's see how he is in the arena."

"I'd settle for seeing him get into his clothes," said Duff. "He must need a shoehorn!"

* * *

At three o'clock in the afternoon the music began, announcing the first act of the tragedy, *The Death of the Bull*. It was the *suerte de varas*, the test by lances. The bull took the opportunity to display his courage. The second act followed, the education of the bull by the *banderilleros*, to slow down the pace, so that the bull's attack was more accurate, more conscious. Finally, the third and last act, the death of the bull, was carried out. And then it was over.

* * *

But not for the crowd. Outside the arena the cafes were packed. In the Iruna, the largest of them, Ernest, Hadley, Harold, Duff, and Pat sat at a round table drinking French champagne and Spanish red wine. Although they'd all had quite a bit to drink, Pat, as usual, was the only one drunk. He looked balefully at his empty glass. Ernest sat next to Duff. She leaned over to him and made herself heard over the noise.

"Recibiendo? What's recibiendo?"

"It means 'to recieve the bull by sword,' " Ernest explained. "The matador provokes the bull to charge, the way you saw Ordoñez do it. And that was a special privilege, an unusually beautiful performance."

"An unusually beautiful boy," said Duff. "And only nineteen years old!"

"Duff, it's the most dangerous, the most arrogant way to kill a bull, and at the same time the most spectacular. A matador has to be a great killer, he has to love to kill, to take pleasure in the kill . . . see the moment as a spiritual climax. A clean kill, an aesthetically pleasing kill, produces a sense of pride, and it's pride that spurs men on to rebel against death. It's pride that makes bullfighting. And the passion to kill . . . makes a great matador."

Harold tried to join the conversation. "Okay, Hem," he said. "It's a tough game."

Ernest's eyes flashed. "A tough game. You call that a tough game? We're talking about death, Harold. About the inevitability of death. A man who rebels against death, who administers death—that's a godlike quality. It's a profound experience."

Harold stared back at Ernest without flinching. His look was one of disgust. Duff pitied him.

"Poor Harold," she said. "It wasn't a fair fight, was it?"

Harold cast Duff a wounded glance. Then he told Hemingway exactly what he thought.

"You know, Hem, the sun was hot out there, so hot all I could do was drink water, glass after glass of water. Then it occurred to me: the bull's thirsty."

"Thirsty?" Ernest spat out the word.

"Thirsty! You think they give the bull any water? Of course not. It might calm him. Everything they do to him is torture, to make him mad, to make him fight! Do you really think they give him water?"

Ernest glared, said nothing.

"Bullfighting disgusts me," said Harold. "It's worse than a public execution. It's the slaughtering of an animal. It's shameful and I was ashamed to be there."

Drunkenly, Pat put in his two cents: "What are you doing here, Harold? Why don't you just clear out! You're not wanted here. We've had our fun with you."

It was Duff's turn to lash out at Harold Loeb.

"You have been very amusing, Harold. But you can go now. Go on. Nobody wants you here."

Pat Guthrie looked around triumphantly. "That's right, isn't it? We don't want him here anymore, do we?"

Silence. Everyone was embarrassed, including Ernest. Pat tried to refill his glass, missed, the wine spilling onto the table. Nobody dared look at Harold, whose hands were trembling. Then he answered quietly, just loud enough to make himself heard over the general din of the cafe Iruna. He stared at Duff.

"I'll go if that's what you want."

For a moment everyone held his breath. Then Ernest exploded.

"You lousy bastard!" he shouted. "Hiding behind a woman's skirt!"

Harold stood, staring straight at Ernest.

"All right!" He nodded toward the open doorway, the street outside. "Let's go!"

Loeb turned and walked from the table. Unconvincingly, Duff held out a hand to stop him, but he ignored it. Ernest got up and followed.

* * *

Ernest and Harold had difficulty making their way past the arcades through the swaying crowd. A large group of people had formed a chain and were dancing. Young people were keeping the rhythm with drums, long slow beats.

They passed through a narrow gate and into a small courtyard. Harold removed his jacket, then his glasses. He folded the side-pieces carefully, put them in his jacket pocket.

"If my glasses get broken there's no place in this entire town I can have them repaired," he said.

Harold was looking for a safe place to put his jacket. He was about to lay it on the ground, but then wrinkled his nose, apparently having smelled something he didn't like. He cleaned off the spot with his foot, put the jacket down. Then he turned, raised both fists, and blinked shortsightedly.

There was a wide grin on Ernest's face. Laughing, he shook his head. "Don't look at me like that, Harold. How am I supposed to hit you if you look at me like that?"

"I don't want to fight," Harold admitted.

"Me neither."

Harold dropped his fists. Ernest picked up his jacket and, holding it like a tailor, invited Harold to put it on. Harold grinned and slipped into the jacket. Ernest clapped him on the shoulder.

"Who cares about some idiot who can't hold his liquor?" he said. "To hell with what Pat says. His balls and his brains have been put through the meat grinder. He's jealous, that's all."

Harold hesitated before answering. He adjusted his glasses, took them off and wiped them, put them back on.

"Well, he doesn't have to be jealous of me," he said. "It's like he said, the fun is over. I expected more from Duff. I'm the one who was stupid."

"You fell in love with an exciting woman," said Ernest. "There's nothing stupid about that."

"We spent a week on the coast together, Hem. I thought it might be the beginning of something. I hoped it would be, but it wasn't. It was just a week on the coast." Harold's voice hardened. He looked at Ernest suspiciously. "What about you? Have you slept with her?"

"No."

"Are you going to?"

Harold looked at Ernest as if he were about to cry. Ernest returned the look briefly, then put his arm around his old friend and began walking. "Let's get drunk, Harold."

"Not this time."

Ernest stopped, faced Harold, who struggled to find his voice.

"Maybe that's what went wrong, Hem," he said, stuttering, gulping air. "Maybe I don't drink enough for her!"

"Maybe."

"Good night, Hem."

Paris—Fall, 1925

Hadley was out strolling with Bumby in the baby carriage. They were in the square in front of the Galerie Fouchard, trendy, chic, and modern, and the fall weather in Paris was magnificent. She leaned over the carriage and smiled down at her son.

"Papa's going hunting, Papa's a good hunter, Papa's going to bring home our dinner," she sang. She was hungry and the song had real meaning.

Ernest sat on a park bench a few yards away. His arms were crossed and he looked lost in thought. A *gendarme* walked slowly past him, raising an eyebrow at Hemingway's shabby clothes.

When the policeman had gone, Hadley edged closer to her husband. A small cluster of pigeons were at Ernest's feet, pecking at birdseed. When she was sure no one was looking, Hadley nodded to Ernest.

Ernest sprang to life, diving for the pigeons, missing.

"Damn," said Ernest Hemingway.

"Well, at least you're a good writer," said his wife.

It began to rain. They ran for cover under the gallery awning, waiting for it to pass. In the window was displayed a large, colorful oil painting by Jean Miro, *The Farm*. It caught their eye, and for a moment they both forgot about eating.

Within the gallery M. Fouchard, the owner, watched them. He straightened his vest expectantly. He bowed courteously as they entered.

"What may I do for you?" he said with a smile.

Hadley pointed to the picture in the window. "We just wanted to know the price of that one."

M. Fouchard took the painting out of the window and set it on an easel illuminated by several spotlights. He said nothing, waiting.

"Isn't it beautiful!" Hadley exclaimed. "Know what, Tatie? I'd like it for my birthday."

Hemingway nodded. "Miro is the only painter who can put together everything you find in Spain when you're there, and everything you can imagine it to be when you're not."

M. Fouchard nodded appreciatively. Ernest looked at him questioningly.

"Well," he said. "What's it cost?"

"Five thousand francs, monsieur."

Ernest bit his lip. Hadley frowned.

"That's more than we have," she said.

"Much more," said Ernest wistfully.

"Maybe when your book comes out . . ."

Ernest nodded. He led Hadley to the door, paused, then turned back to M. Fouchard.

"We'll be back," he said.

* * *

Hadley and Pauline Pfeiffer sat on a bench by the carousel in the Jardin de Luxembourg, bare now of leaves and flowers. They watched Bumby riding on a wooden horse, round and round, happy and waving to them. Hadley skimmed through a fashion magazine that Pauline had brought along. Pauline posed a question.

"When I was in Italy," she began, "someone told me that Ernest was wounded in the war and got a medal for bravery. True?"

"Yes. He was badly wounded, both legs. He spent two months in a hospital in Milan. They called him 'the Kid.' He was only nineteen. He fell in love with one of the nurses."

"Oh?"

"He was determined to marry her, but she decided for someone else. He's never really gotten over it—being dumped by a woman."

Pauline paused for a moment, looked at the carousel. Then, "Has he had lots of women?"

Hadley shook her head and laughed. "I think the girl on the pier in Michigan was his first. And all the others—just talk. Ernest has always been good at making up stories."

"I read that story," said Pauline. "He really seems to have a feeling for women."

Hadley finished skimming through the magazine. She handed it back to Pauline. "So many beautiful things in there," she said. She stood, staring longingly at the barren trees.

Pauline took her arm. "I've a splendid idea," she said. "I've got to attend a fashion show; it's Coco Chanel's newest collection. I'm doing a piece on it for Vogue. Why don't you come with me? It'll be fun! And afterwards we can go to the pictures."

Hadley nodded toward Bumby. "What will I do with him?"

"Deposit him."

On their way to the fashion show they passed the Galerie Fouchard. Pauline, carrying Bumby, paused to look at the paintings. Hadley looked for the Miro, and it was there, but to her utter disappointment there was a tag at the bottom which read *"vendu."*

"But that's impossible!" said Hadley. "Just a few days ago he said . . ."

She did not finish her sentence. Her disappointment had turned to fury. She opened the door and walked determinedly into the shop.

* * *

In the cafe Closerie des Lilas Hemingway sat at his usual spot, talking to Scott Fitzgerald, young, good-looking with blond wavy hair, high forehead, lively, friendly eyes. The waiter opened a bottle of Veuve Cliquot champagne, poured two glasses.

Fitzgerald took a sip from his glass, put it down. "I'd like you to read my new book, *The Great Gatsby*," he said.

"When can I have it?"

"I lent it to someone. My last copy. As soon as it's back you can read it. Maxwell Perkins wrote to me. He says it's not selling well."

Hemingway shook his head. "But the reviews were excellent."

"Right. The reviews couldn't have been better. They could only have been better if the reviewers wrote better."

Scott was drinking much too fast. He tossed down one glass of champagne after another. Suddenly small beads of sweat began to appear on his upper lip. His face became pale. The waiter stared at him, came over to the table and spoke quietly to Ernest.

"Does he not feel well, monsieur?"

"He's all right."

"Monsieur Fitzgerald looks like he's going to die," said the waiter.

"No," said Ernest. "Alcohol always affects him like that." Carefully, thoughtfully, with wide, flourishing strokes, he covered the page of his notebook with sentences.

"'Oh, Jake,' he read aloud to no one, 'we could have had such a damn good time together.' Ahead was a mounted policeman in khaki, directing traffic. He raised his baton. The car slowed, suddenly pressing Brett against me. 'It's damn nice to think so,' I said."

He stared at the last sentence, slowly nodding. He

looked up when his name was called. Hadley, carrying Bumby, entered the cafe with Pauline just behind.

"Bad news, Tatie," said Hadley, sitting next to him. "We passed by Fouchard's gallery. He's sold our painting! And do you know who bought it? Of all people, your friend, Evan Shipman."

Hemingway sat back. "But I thought he was broke, too."

"He talked Fouchard into letting him pay in installments."

Ernest shrugged. "Sorry, Hash. You'll have to pick out something else for your birthday."

Quietly, Pauline seated Bumby next to his father. Amazed, Ernest regarded the small boy as if for the first time.

Hadley kissed Ernest's cheek. "As a consolation, Pauline has invited me to a fashion show," she said.

"And you're elected to look after Bumby," said Pauline.

"Hey!" Ernest barked. "What's the big idea?"

Hadley turned around and laughed. "Bye! Have a good time. Oh, and after the show we're going to the pictures!"

When they'd gone the waiter appeared. Ernest looked down at his son questioningly. "Well," he said, "what'll it be, kid? A beer, or would you prefer a little absinthe?"

Bumby blinked.

"Bring monsieur an ice cream," Ernest said to the waiter. "The doctor told him to lay off the liquor for a while. It's his liver, you know." Then he looked at his notebook, crossed out the last line, and wrote another: *"Yes," I said. "Isn't it pretty to think so?"*

Slowly, carefully, he wrote the question mark at the end of the sentence. He turned to Bumby when the ice cream arrived.

"That's better, eh?" and then, to the waiter, he asked, "What's today's date, Jean?"

"Twenty-one September."

Ernest wrote down the date. "The end," he wrote in his notebook.

"Jean? If Mr. Shipman shows up could you tell him to get in touch? It's important."

* * *

Later that evening Ernest and Evan Shipman sat across from each other at a marble-topped table in a corner, shooting dice. Bumby was watching.

"My mother always told me," said Hemingway, "trust in God . . . and never shoot craps on a blanket. Sixteen, Shipman. Your turn."

He pushed the dice to Shipman, who shook the leather cup and shot. "Thirteen. Damn!"

Ernest shot, wrote down the score on a piece of paper.

"Keep this up and you've as good as won," said Shipman.

Ernest shot, wrote down the score, rubbed his hands.

"Why the hell do you want it so badly, Ernest?" Shipman asked. No answer. He shot, not enough. Ernest drew a line, added everything up. He stood and received Shipman's congratulations.

Bumby ate his third plate of ice cream.

* * *

Late that evening Ernest and Bumby huddled in Bumby's room listening to Hadley and Pauline as they entered the apartment on rue Notre Dame des Champs. When they heard Hadley squeal, they burst into the living room. Both women were staring, flabbergasted, at the Miro painting hanging on the wall.

"Happy birthday!" Ernest shouted, hugging his wife.

She kissed him, hardly able to tear her eyes from the picture. "Oh, Ernest, that's the most beautiful, the most thoughtful surprise you could have given me. But how on earth did you get it?"

"You'll never guess," said Ernest.

* * *

Later that night Pauline gave Bumby a bath. The little boy sat in the bathtub, squealing merrily. Ernest, leafing through a Bible, watched her from the living room. His notebooks lay about on the table amid a clutter of pens, pencils, erasers, and wineglasses. Hadley came out of the kitchen with a prewarmed bath towel. Ernest looked at her thoughtfully, nodded to his manuscript.

"The bullfighter is important," he said, "but he's not the main character. There's an English woman, Brett Ashley, who wears men's hats, and an American journalist, Jake Barnes, who was wounded in the war. He's impotent. They meet in Paris. She loves men, spends her nights carousing with a young Scot who doesn't have any money and can't decide if he's queer or not. And then there's Jake's friend who studied at Princeton, a Jew, who falls head over heels in love with Brett. What do you think?"

Hadley shrugged. "Duff Twysden, Pat Guthrie, Harold . . . you?"

"Took me eight weeks and seven notebooks. Ninety thousand words. The hardest job I ever had. In all fairness, you two ladies could exert yourselves a little. What do you think of *River to the Sea?*"

Hadley spoke quickly. "So far I like *Fiesta* best."

"You can't compare them."

"You asked me what I thought. That's what I think."

"I don't like the title. What about *Lost Generation?*"

Hadley thought for a moment. "Sounds pretty good. But I like *Fiesta* better."

"*Fiesta*'s no good, Hash. I don't want a foreign word for the title."

Pauline, who had been following the conversation, entered the room. "*Lost Generation?*" she asked. "What's that?"

"An expression. It was coined by Gertrude Stein. She balled us out with it. She said we're a lost generation, all of us who were in the war. Remember, Hash?"

Hadley was drying Bumby. "How could I? She doesn't speak with wives," she said curtly.

Ernest found a passage in the Bible. "Hey, how's this sound? 'Vanity of vanities, says the preacher. All is vanity. What does a man gain by all his toil—"

Pauline put her hand on his arm. She knew the passage by heart and recited it to the end. "All his toil under the sun. One generation passes away and another generation comes, but the Earth abideth forever. The sun also rises and the sun goes down, and hastens to his place where he arose."

Ernest looked at Pauline. "The sun also rises," he said softly.

* * *

A little later Ernest accompanied Pauline down to the street to hail a taxi.

"When may I read it?" she asked.

"Well, it's really not finished yet. I have to go through the whole thing again. Not right away. I'll get on it when I'm back in the mountains this winter. So much passion, you know. It can really tire a man out."

"And they're all in it? Harold Loeb? Kitty? Lady Duff?"

"Every single one. I tear them all apart. And Loeb, he's the villain."

"And the rest of us?"

"I left you out."

"Oh?" Pauline was disappointed, but tried not to show it.

"Well, you didn't fit in, Pauline."

"And Hadley? Is Hadley in it?"

"I don't write about Hadley."

"Because she's your wife?"

"Because she's Hadley."

Pauline looked down at the cobbled street for a moment. Then, pulling herself together, she looked at him and smiled.

"What do you think?" she asked. "Will I fit into your next novel?"

"I don't know."

She offered him her small hand and he took it.

"Maybe it's too early to tell," she said.

Swiss Alps—Winter, 1925/1926

The yellow bus coughed and sputtered up the mountain road, stopping at the post station. Waiting for it were Ernest, with Bumby on his shoulders, and Hadley, holding her husband's hand. They waved when Pauline appeared on the platform. Wearing the latest winter sportswear creations, she attracted a lot of attention from the other vacationers, Ernest especially.

"How I've missed you!" she said, hugging Ernest, Hadley and Bumby all at once. "My God, look how big Bumby's become!"

"Good peasant stock," Ernest joked.

The hotel servant loaded the sleigh with Pauline's baggage, which included two trunks and four suitcases. They all jumped aboard and with a crack of the whip the driver set out for the hotel, a small quiet chalet on the other side of the broad valley basin.

It snowed every day, right up to Christmas, and the trio grew closer than ever before. Leaving Bumby with a trusted hotel maid, Ernest, Hadley, and Pauline skied every day. In a few weeks they were tan and in perfect form, a happy, laughing party that never seemed to stop.

One morning at breakfast the hotel proprietor appeared at their table with a large tray. On it was their favorite breakfast food, a huge portion of *Kaiserschmarr'n*.

"Dig in, ladies," said Ernest. "It's going to be a strenuous day!"

But Hadley couldn't eat. "Tatie," she said, "there's something wrong with Bumby. I've called the doctor."

"I heard him coughing in the night," said Pauline. "All the way from my room."

"I think it's whooping cough," said Hadley.

"But you'll still come skiing with us?" Pauline asked.

"I'd like to. But I think I better stay with Bumby."

Ernest and Pauline exchanged glances.

"We'll miss you," said Pauline.

* * *

A short time later Ernest and Pauline, trudging up a snow-covered slope, stopped at a hay shed to strip the skins from the bottoms of their skis. A hot sun shone down from an azure sky, casting a sharp clear light on everything below.

"You know, Turgenev didn't write the greatest books," said Hemingway, "but he was the greatest writer. Ever read a story of his called 'It's Rattling'?"

Pauline shook her head.

"It's in the second volume of *A Sportsman's Sketches*. I'll give it to you."

"I finally finished *War and Peace*," she said. "Great book."

"Can you imagine what kind of a book it would have been if Turgenev had written it?"

"No, I can't."

"Chekhov. He wrote about six good stories, but Chekhov was an amateur writer," said Ernest.

"And Tolstoy?"

"A prophet."

"Maupassant?"

"A professional writer."

"Balzac?"

"Definitely professional."

"Okay," she said, facing him and smiling. "What's a professional writer?"

Ernest laughed. "A writer who gets rich with one book, and finishes a new one each spring."

She looked down, pretending to adjust her bindings. "What about you, Ernest? Are you a pro?"

"Not yet, fortunately."

They sat quietly for a minute. Ernest sighed.

"Liveright sent me a telegram."

"I thought you had something on your mind," she said.

"Yeah. They've turned down *Torrents of Spring*."

"Because you made fun of Sherwood Anderson."

"Maybe, I don't know. But Scribner's is interested. That means I have to go to New York in the next few days to meet with Max Perkins, the editor. You'll stay here with Hadley, won't you?"

Pauline, taken by surprise, flushed. "Of course," she replied, almost too quickly. Hiding her disappointment, she tried to change the subject.

"May I ask you something? You don't have to answer."

"Go ahead," said Ernest good-naturedly. "Shoot."

"What makes you happy?"

Ernest reflected for a moment. They got up. He looked around: the horizon, the snow-covered mountains all about them, the blue sky, the sun. Hemingway gestured to all of it with his ski pole, smiled.

"No," said Pauline, looking doubtful. "That's not what I mean."

"Okay. Two private *Barrera* seats in a big bullfighting arena and a trout stream all to myself."

Pauline shook her head. "What else?"

"Oh, two charming houses in the city—one where I'd have my wife and children, where I'd live monogamously and love them sincerely. And another one where I'd keep my beautiful mistresses on nine different floors."

"You're making fun of me," she said.

Annoyed, she pushed off and skied down the slope, followed by Ernest. Suddenly she disappeared behind a mound. He heard her cry out and hurried to her. She lay in the snow, one ski off and the other dangling. He knelt beside her and in a moment she was on her feet. She held him tightly.

"You're trembling," he said.

Pauline closed her eyes. Their faces came closer and closer. They kissed, tenderly at first, cautiously, then more and more passionately.

"I love you," she whispered, "I love you."

Slowly they sank to the snow, exchanging kisses, caresses.

"Take me with you to New York," she begged. "I can't bear to be without you. I need time with you . . . alone."

Ernest freed himself. Torn, he thought carefully, then looked into her eyes.

"Not New York," he said. "Paris. I'll meet you in Paris . . . before I come back here." He took her again into his strong arms and held her tightly. "I promise."

* * *

Five days later Ernest sat across a desk from Max Perkins in the editorial offices of Charles Scribner's Publishing House on Fifth Avenue, New York. Perkins was all business.

"Fifteen hundred dollars. *The Torrents of Spring* is a good book, Ernest. I like the way you've taken aim at Anderson's weaknesses: his refined style, the naive sexual promiscuity of his characters . . . of course you know all that yourself. In addition, you'll receive fifteen percent of the profits. I think it's a fair offer."

Ernest nodded. "Fifteen hundred in advance. That's for *Torrents* and *The Sun Also Rises*?"

"Correct. Send me the proofs of *Torrents*. I'm not quite finished with *Sun Also Rises*."

Hemingway tried to disguise his excitement. Looking around the cluttered office, his eyes fell on a framed photograph of Scott Fitzgerald.

"I'd like a place next to him someday," he said.

"That can be arranged," said Perkins.

"How is he?"

"Started a new book," said the editor. "Doesn't see anyone, isn't drinking, working hard. We sold the film rights for *Gatsby*, fifteen thousand. He hopes that'll hold him till spring."

"If he needs money, take it out of my royalties and send it to him," said Ernest with a grin. "Maybe he'll get the Nobel Prize someday."

"If they ever award it to an American," said Perkins.

Hemingway stood, shook his editor's hand. "Scott's the only one I'd like to see get it," he said.

Alone in the elevator Ernest's excitement overcame him. Holding both fists above his head, he closed his eyes and laughed all the way to the ground floor.

* * *

Pauline was waiting for him on the platform of the Gare de Lyon in Paris. When the train pulled in, she found him struggling with two suitcases and a portable typewriter. They fell into each other's arms.

"I missed you so much," she said. "I missed you indecently."

Together they gathered up his luggage and walked down the long platform, out of the station.

In the taxi, they did not speak.

The late afternoon light bathed Pauline's apartment with gold. Outside, the sounds of passersby in the rue Picot could be faintly heard.

In the bedroom, Ernest was making love to Pauline. He held her tightly, protectively, domineeringly. Her beauty enchanted him.

A short time later they lay in bed, covered by a silk sheet. On their sides, facing each other, they spoke seriously.

"You know, I have to go back to Hadley. I've already been away much too long. She'll be worried."

Tenderly she ran her fingers through his hair. There were tears in her eyes.

"If only we could stay together like this forever," she cried. "What are you going to tell her?"

Slowly he shook his head. "I don't know."

She closed her eyes. "I'm so ashamed."

He put his arms around her, holding her tightly as she buried her face in his chest and cried softly.

"Don't ever forget, Pauline, that I love you, too."

Outside, night fell. With it came a light rain. They listened to the rain as it pattered on the balcony, then fell asleep.

* * *

The moment Ernest stepped off the post bus, Hadley was on him, hugging, covering his face with kisses. There were tears in her eyes.

"Oh, Tatie, we thought you were coming last week!"

"It was . . . unavoidable," he said, looking away. Bumby came running across the snow and jumped into his arms. He looked healthy, stocky, with rosy cheeks.

"Papa!"

Ernest hugged his son and tried to swallow the lump in his throat.

* * *

That night Ernest sat at a table in front of their hotel room window, correcting a typewritten manuscript. Now and then he looked up from his work at the snow-covered landscape, bathed in moonlight—almost as bright as day.

He sensed, rather than heard, Hadley standing behind him. He turned and looked at her. She wore a bathrobe and it was obvious that she'd been waiting half the night for him to come to bed. He tried to put down the manuscript, tried and tried, but couldn't. Now it was too late.

"You'll ruin your eyes," she said, not looking at him.

He tried to brighten. "I dedicated it to you and Bumby," he said softly. "*The Sun Also Rises*, for Hadley and John Hadley Nicanor."

She said nothing, her eyes on the floor. Then she looked up.

"You love her," she said flatly.

Stung, Ernest twinged. Hadley held up her hand.

"No! No, Ernest, don't say anything. You don't have to justify yourself. I felt it, that she loves you. I just want to know . . . if you love her."

He stood. "Hash," he begged, "please, don't insist, don't wreck everything."

"Did . . . you sleep with her?"

Ernest looked down, then slowly raised his head. He was furious.

"You're going to destroy everything," he said.

"*I have to know!*"

"Do you want to leave me?" he asked. "Call it quits? Is that what you want?" He slammed his fist on the table. "Damn it!" he thundered. "Why did you have to say it?"

He stepped toward her and for a moment she thought he would strike her. But then he walked by her without a word. She watched him go.

"Ernest, please!"
No reply. She began to cry.

Paris—Spring, 1926

Morning, a quiet time in the Gare de Lyon. Ernest, Hadley, and Bumby stepped off the train. A porter took their baggage, and they followed. At the taxi stand Hadley addressed her husband, almost formally.

"Bumby and I will move into a hotel."

"Why?"

"I don't want to stay in the apartment alone. Too many ghosts."

"Which hotel?"

"Maybe the Beauvoir. Across from the Closerie des Lilas."

"My cafe?"

She nodded. "If they've a room on the street side I could watch if you're writing out on the terrace."

He studied his feet. She offered him her hand.

"What happens now?" she asked.

"I don't know," he said. "I have to think, Hadley. I need time."

A taxi pulled up, the door opened. Hadley and Bumby got in.

"Take care," he said, waving as the taxi pulled out of the station. Hadley did not look back, but Bumby leaned out the window and waved until the taxi passed from sight.

Ernest remained motionless on the platform. At his feet were a suitcase, his Corona portable typewriter, and his skis.

* * *

That evening, in Pauline's spacious apartment on rue Picot, Ernest lay naked under white silk sheets.

Pauline lay beside him, staring at the ceiling. He could feel her trembling, knew what was coming.

"It's impossible," she said at last. "We can't go on this way. You'll have to break it off with her."

He shut his eyes. "I can't," he said. "Not yet."

"You love her."

He sat up in bed, looked down at her. "Pauline," he began, "it's not all that long ago I was working for the *Toronto Star*. I had to cover a peace conference in Lausanne, and Hadley joined me. She packed all my manuscripts in a little suitcase. She wanted to surprise me. The suitcase was stolen at the train station. All my early work, short stories, poems, sketches, were gone. I had to start all over again from scratch. Hadley tried to tell me what had happened, but she couldn't. She just cried and cried. I tried to console her. I told her that whatever happened, it couldn't be that bad. She finally told me. I've never seen anyone suffer as much as she did."

"You love her."

* * *

A few days later Ernest and Scott Fitzgerald sat on a park bench in the Jardin de Luxembourg, which was just beginning to come alive with spring. It was a gray day, not many children, and the mothers who were there looked at the two writers suspiciously. They looked a little shabby, almost like tramps, each drinking red wine from his own bottle.

Scott slapped Ernest's knee. "*Fiesta*'s going to be a success, Hem," he said. "Really. The characters are so alive, so full of irony, losers and winners at one and the same time."

Ernest laughed. "I'm going to ask the publishers to add an epigram: *The Sun Also Rises*, written with the support of F. Scott Fitzgerald, prophet of the Jazz Age."

"Now, that's very generous." Scott had another hit of wine. So did Ernest.

"Honestly, Scott, your comments were a great help. You told me to get rid of all that biographical stuff, let it flow into the story. It made a big difference."

Fitzgerald was silent; then, "It's ultimately a very tragic story. The way all people go to hell," he said sadly.

"Yeah." They both had another drink.

"How's Hadley?"

Ernest shrugged. "Our life together is all washed up. She's been wonderful. It's all my fault. I feel like hell." He looked at his bottle, half empty. "Well, since it's a hell of my own making I guess I might as well enjoy it." He held up the wine, toasted the fountain, drank.

"The world is so full of a number of things, I'm sure we should all be happy as kings," said Scott Fitzgerald.

"Who said that?"

"Stevenson."

"Right."

Hemingway emptied his bottle.

"Scott, tell me something."

"What?"

"How happy are kings?"

Scott handed his bottle to his friend.

"Drink, Hem. You're thirstier. Tell me something. Did you and Hadley sleep together before you were married?"

"I don't know."

"What do you mean you don't know?"

"I can't remember."

"How can you not remember something like that?" Scott asked.

"I don't know. Odd, isn't it?"

"Worse than odd."

"Worse."

Scott leaned toward him. "You know," he said, "I've never slept with anyone besides Zelda."

"I didn't know."

"I thought I'd told you."

"Nope, Scott. You told me a lot of things. But not that."

Scott looked at his lap, shrugged. "Zelda told me that the way I was built I could never make any woman happy. That's what first threw me off balance. She said it was a matter of measurements. I haven't felt the same since she said that."

Ernest finished the second bottle, put it on the ground, and faced his friend. "Look, Scott, you're perfectly fine. When you look at yourself from above, you seem to come up short. Go over to the Louvre and take a look at the statues. Then go home and look at yourself in the mirror."

"The statues might not be normal."

Hemingway laughed. "Most people would settle for them!"

* * *

A week passed, then another. One day Ernest received a telegram from Hadley, asking that he meet her, with Pauline, at their old apartment on the rue Notre Dame des Champs.

It was a bright spring day, the sun hot over Paris, but the light was gloomy in the apartment. Shades were drawn and, with the exception of some rented furniture, the rooms were nearly empty. Hadley sat at the table, wearing her jacket. Ernest and Pauline sat across from her.

"I want us all to face up to the situation," said Hadley.

Pauline tried to catch her eye. "Hadley," she said imploringly, "I promise you I never set out to . . . I only wanted to be your friend. That's the truth."

Hadley ignored her. "We have to settle this," she

said. "There is also the child to consider. Do you love each other?"

At first Ernest and Pauline just stared into space. Then they looked at each other.

"I love him," said Pauline. She took his hand.

"I love her," said Ernest.

Hadley nodded, dry-eyed. "You're Catholic, Pauline," she said. "You're a practicing Catholic. I assume you want to marry him."

Ernest spoke for her: "Yes, we want to get married."

Hadley took a folded piece of paper from her handbag, put it on the table in front of them.

"I've come to a decision. If you and Pauline agree to split up for one hundred days, and if at the end of that time you are still in love and still want to marry, I'll give you a divorce. Here it is in writing. I've signed it. It's up to you."

Hadley got up from the table and went to the window. She could hear scratching sounds behind her as they signed the paper.

* * *

That evening Ernest took Pauline to the Gare de Lyon. He carried her suitcases to her compartment, helped her in. Nervously, he kept looking at the big clock over the *Train Bleu* restaurant inside the station. She squeezed his arm.

"I'll miss you so," she said.

"A hundred days. That's three months. It's not eternity."

She shook her head. "Only a quarter year. It'll go by quickly."

Ernest looked at the ceiling. "I don't know, Pauline. Maybe this is a mistake. Maybe we should go off somewhere together. I wonder if getting Hadley's consent is worth the pain of separation."

Pauline was strong-willed. "No," she said. "We

have to show her, prove to her, that our love is stronger than hers. Otherwise we forfeit our right. Our love justifies what we're doing to her. That's the only way I can look at it, Hem."

Ernest looked at the clock again. She took his hands and held on to them.

"Don't worry," she said. "I'll read lots, I'll relax, get healthy and strong, and everything will be fine. As soon as I'm on the ship I'll write to you. And when we see each other again, we'll be one, you and me, the same person. I love you more than ever, Ernest. I'll never give you up, I swear."

The south-bound train began to move. Ernest took a few steps along with her, then she let go of his hands. They waved. The train slowly pulled out of the station.

PART

TWO

East Africa—Winter, 1933

The sun, already low over the expansive savanna of the Serengeti, was still bright and gold-yellow above the huge Ngorongoro crater. Looming like a mirage, far in the distance, was the white cone of Kilimanjaro. Antelopes, zebras, and gnus grazed peacefully together, but alert, keeping an eye out for lions.

Ernest Hemingway sat in a camp chair in the shade of a large acacia, reading Tolstoy's *Sevastopol*. He closed the book for a moment of quiet reflection. Things were not so bad. Hadley was lost in the distant pass, the pain and hurt gone, a new life with Pauline begun. Her wealth had enabled them to return to America, build a house in Key West, and bring two children into the world. He could see Bumby practically whenever he liked, and knew that in the future they would be even closer. And then there was his career. *The Sun Also Rises,* a huge success, was nearly eclipsed by his second novel, *A Farewell to Arms,* which had been made into a Hollywood movie. His was a carefree life.

No, not quite carefree. In the past two years tensions had built up in their marriage. Pauline had changed, or at least he thought so. The passions of their early romance were no longer there, and he missed them. But it was more than that. Had her wealth and his success made life too easy? He'd had to find out, test himself, and that was why they were in Africa.

Waving away a small cloud of mosquitoes, he took a notebook from his bag and jotted down a few lines, then read them aloud to himself.

His words described the feelings of a man who

loved the landscape of Africa, who expressed his happiness at returning there. The man explained that he enjoyed living in such a place—a place where he likes the natives and where there is game and plenty of birds.

He paused, looked over at Pauline, who was curled up asleep on her leather jacket. The atmosphere was peaceful, almost pastoral. M'Cola, one of their black gun bearers, squatted on his haunches, peering at the plain.

He wrote another line expressing how the country made the man happy in the same way being with a woman he loved made him happy.

"That's very nice," said Pauline, stretching her arms above her head.

"Sleep well?" he asked.

"Better than in the finest hotels."

"I like watching you when you sleep," he said. "You curl up just like an animal that knows it's out of danger."

"I am out of danger. As long as you and M'Cola are looking out for me."

Sitting up, she looked at the sun. "It's late."

"Percival should be back any time now," Ernest said. "The sun's perfect. Time to finally get down to some hunting."

A loud roar issued from the savanna. Ernest reached for his rifle. M'Cola stood.

"*Simba,*" said the gun bearer.

"*Wapi?*"

M'Cola pointed toward the plain. Ernest beckoned to Pauline. "That was a lion."

Pauline tensed, staring into the distance. Suddenly there was a crackling sound nearby, the sound of branches breaking. Pauline froze.

From behind a bush appeared the white hunter, Philip Percival, and their friend, all smiles. Pauline quickly recovered from her fright.

"You were afraid," said Ernest.

"Damned fear."

"There's a Somali proverb that says: 'A brave man is afraid of a lion three times: when he spots his trail, when he hears him roar the first time, and when he meets him face-to-face.'"

"And what does your Somali proverb say about a brave woman?" she inquired.

"That she doesn't have to worry," said Ernest. "Because I'll protect her."

Pauline laughed. She ran her hand through her husband's hair as if he were a little boy.

Charles, Percival, and another gun bearer, Charo, arrived at the camp, tense, excited.

"We saw it," said Thompson. "A real beauty with a pitch black mane."

"Where?" Hemingway was on his feet.

"About two miles from here."

"Damn good lion," said Percival.

Ernest nodded. "Then let's go get him."

A short time later they all piled out of the Land-Rover and moved down a small hill of brush and tall grass. Percival scanned the horizon with his binoculars, then handed them to Ernest.

"Over there by that fruit tree," whispered the white hunter.

Ernest was so excited that the binocular lenses fogged up. He wiped them with his kerchief. "Yes," he said, "I see him. Big head. Incredibly yellow. What an animal! So majestic, so calm and mighty. He's spectacular." He handed the glasses to Pauline. "Do you see him?" He held her shoulders.

"My God!" Pauline exclaimed. "He's huge! Do we have to shoot him?"

He looked at her seriously. "That's what we paid for," he said.

Ernest looked at Percival expectantly. The white hunter looked at his watch, then up at the sun. He took

Pauline's rifle, loaded it, checked the action, handed it back to her.

"He's yours," he said flatly. "You have first shot. If he attacks, you have to go for him. You have to be ready to shoot yourself out of any trouble you shoot yourself into. That's the first rule of big-game hunting. And don't try anything fancy. A lion can do a hundred yards faster than it takes to get off two good shots. Then he's on top of you."

"Where should I aim?"

"Go for the breast, in the neck, shoot him in the spine. Shoot him dead. Take your time, get good aim. It's the first hit that counts."

The lion was coming nearer. "How close should I let him get?" Pauline asked.

"Hard to tell." Percival was whispering now. "The lion's got a say in that. Ninety yards would be a fair range. But remember: if you miss, the bastard's up for grabs."

Percival turned and signaled to M'Cola. Pauline moved forward slowly, in a crouch. M'Cola, carrying a short-barreled Mannlicher, followed close behind, with Ernest and Percival on his flanks and Charles bringing up the rear. Ernest carried a Springfield, the safety off, ready to shoot.

The lion appeared in a clearing, looking at them. Pauline raised the Mannlicher, safety released. She dropped to one knee. The gun bearer crouched next to her. Pauline tried to breathe evenly. At that second the lion leaped toward cover.

"Nail him!" said Percival.

Pauline fired. The lion leaped in Ernest's direction. "Watch out!"

Ernest shouldered the Springfield, aimed and fired. The lion collapsed, tumbled over, lay still. Ernest fired a second shot which struck the sandy ground in front of the outstretched beast, sending a fountain of sand into the air. The hunters approached carefully. M'Cola picked up a stone and threw it at the lion to see if it was really dead. It was.

Charo flashed a white-toothed smile at Ernest. "Good shot, B'wana! *Piga muzuri!*" Then he ran over to shake Pauline's hand.

Ernest was confused, shaken. He looked at his friend. "Did you shoot?"

"Hell no, Hem. I was just about to when you did."

Charo brought the camera and everyone posed behind the dead lion. Pauline knelt and ran her hand through its golden yellow fur.

"A magnificent animal," she said. Then she looked up at Ernest. "I'm not sure I hit him."

"Just the same," he said consolingly, "it's yours. It's your first lion."

M'Cola looked at Pauline, then at Ernest. He was angry. Pointing to Pauline, then the lion, he exclaimed, *"Mama! Mama piga simba!"*

Ernest shook his head and turned away.

* * *

Camp was set up under the trees at a watering place, several tents around a big camp fire. The hunting party returned, carrying the lion, whose huge paws were tied around a pole so that its head hung to the ground. M'Cola let out a shrill flood of words, spoken quickly, always ending with the word *simba*.

"Mama!" he shouted. *"Mama piga simba! Mama piga simba!"*

The carriers, cooks, skinners, and camp boys rushed from the camp and surrounded Pauline. Picking her up on their shoulders, they carried her into the camp triumphantly, then put her down in front of her tent.

They all sang, *"Hay, ha Mama! Mama piga simba!"*

Percival congratulated her. "You got him, I'm sure. M'Cola said he'd kill anyone who said you didn't."

Pauline beamed. "I feel marvelous. They don't make a habit of carrying me around on their shoulders back home."

"We'll carry you all the way back home on our shoulders," said Charles.

Standing a little off to the side, Ernest was watching the congratulations sullenly. He pulled himself together and went to his wife.

"I really think it was your shot that brought him down," he said.

"Don't lie," she replied with a shrug. "You know it wasn't. But just this once I'd like to enjoy my triumph anyway."

Ernest nodded, turned away.

* * *

That evening Molo, one of the boys, took the big black caldron from the fire and carried it to the bathing tent. He filled the zinc bathtub, tested the water temperature with his fingers, tidied up the soap, sponge, and towels. He failed to notice the small green-and-yellow striped snake hidden in the folds of one of the towels. He returned to the fire where Ernest and the others were sitting around a camp table having drinks.

"*Bathi, Bwana,*" said Molo.

"I'm too tired," said Ernest. "Bathe yourself."

Molo shook his head. "*Bathi, Bwana.*"

"Okay. I'll have a drink first, then I'll *bathi.*"

Pauline, wearing a blue bathrobe and mosquito boots, gave him a gentle push. "You have a drink when you get out," she said. "The water's so nice and warm and murky. Now go on and have your bath."

With a growl and a glass in hand, Ernest removed himself to the bathing tent. He got in the shallow tub, lathered himself from head to toe, then spilled water over his head with the big sponge. Spluttering and spitting, he enjoyed himself heartily until some strong soap got in his eyes.

As he felt around blindly for a bath towel the snake glided over the back of his hand. For a brief second Ernest just sat there, paralyzed. Then he screamed. Lying next to him on a wooden stool was his father's revolver. Ernest grabbed it, cocked the hammer and fired in the direction of the snake.

At that moment Percival rushed into the tent. In a flash, he grabbed the snake behind its head, held it up for Ernest to see. When he'd wiped the soap from his eyes, Ernest looked at the reptile. He shivered, frightened and repulsed.

"God, I hate them," he said. "They petrify me."

Percival, who had been drinking, held the snake closer.

"Touch it!" he ordered.

Hemingway looked away.

"Touch it, you coward!"

Ernest shook his head. "No," he said. "It's not cowardice. It's fear, but a different kind of fear. The kind you can't overcome."

"Rubbish!" shouted the white hunter. "Come on, touch the bloody thing and don't make such a fuss."

Ernest gritted his teeth. He gagged and snarled. Then he grabbed the snake, holding it behind its head the way Percival had.

"You see?" said Percival. "Completely harmless."

Ernest held the snake at arm's length. He looked at it, disgusted and repulsed. "Get it . . . out of here," he snarled.

Percival laughed, took the snake, and put it in the palm of his hand. The snake slunk up his arm, settled on his shoulder.

"Just another goddamn animal," he said.

* * *

The moon was up when the hunters assembled in the dining tent. Under the canvas roof was a large table, already set with silver candelabrum, crystal glasses, and the finest porcelain. Ernest, Pauline, Percival, and Charles took their seats and waited as the boys brought in roast gazelle, corn on the cob, mashed potatoes, wine, and beer. The night was warm, the air full of cicadas chirping. Outside, from the savanna, came the hyenas' curious laughter, then, ominously, the roar of a lion. Frightened, Pauline looked out into the darkness.

Percival raised his glass to her. "You shot him dead today," he said with pride.

"He flipped over like a hare," Charles explained.

Ernest nodded. "You got him all right."

Pauline blushed. "I was on the verge of dropping my rifle and running off."

They ate in silence. Then, as the boys were clearing the table, Percival sat back and lit a cigar.

"Today's hunt reminds me of a story," he said.

Hemingway cocked an eyebrow, leaning closer.

"There was this rich couple. A white hunter went out with them to shoot some lions. When the time came, the husband ran away from the lion. He just ran. His wife scorned him."

Ernest nodded while Percival took another pull on the cigar and continued.

"That night the rich man's wife went to the white hunter's tent. She spent the night. The next day the husband fell apart. He'd lost all his self-respect. He didn't hold it against the white hunter, but he began to hate his wife. Why did he hate her? Because now she knew: she knew he was a coward. She had him right where she wanted him: under her thumb."

Just then there was a commotion in the camp. Two natives, an old man with a bow and quiver and a tall Masai warrior, approached the camp fire. The Masai stood on one leg, scratching the hollow of his knee with his big toe. The old man spoke to M'Cola and Charo, seriously, slowly, without gesturing. Ernest asked Percival, who spoke the language, what was going on.

"He says they've found kudus."

Ernest and Charles jumped to their feet. "Where?"

"A day's walk. Three or four hours by car."

"How many?" Ernest demanded.

"Several. Big kudu bucks. He's left a few men there to watch them."

Hemingway looked at the old hunter and the warrior. "We've heard it before," he said suspiciously. "What do you think?"

"Well," said the white hunter, "they lie like the devil. But this one seems pretty sure of himself. I say we leave at dawn. How's your stomach, Ernest? Are you up to it?"

Ernest, who had been suffering from dysentery for the last twenty-four hours, shook his head. "We'll go, of course. I'm not going to let a case of the runs stop me from bagging one or two kudus."

"You're sure?"

"Dear friends," said Ernest, raising a tall glass of warm beer, "I am damned fine. This calls for a drink!"

"I don't want a drink," said Charles. "I want a kudu! And that's why I'm off to bed. Good night, all." He got up and disappeared into the darkness. Ernest poured himself a glass of whiskey.

Percival looked at him. "You should hit the sack, too, you old African," he said good-naturedly. "Good night."

Ernest looked at him. "But you didn't finish your story," he said.

"Another time."

After he had gone, Ernest downed the whiskey in

one gulp. Suddenly, gripping his stomach and gasping for air, he doubled over. Pauline rushed to him.

"Darling," she said, wiping his brow, "the whiskey just makes it worse."

He shook his head. "Best home remedy there is for the runs. Pour me another."

"You should stop now, dear," she said.

"You should stop giving me advice."

She paused, then spoke again, softly. "You're sick and I'm worried about you. It's been one thing after another for the last two weeks. I think we should get you to a doctor."

Hemingway raised himself and refilled his glass.

"Pauline, I'm just a big jerk with a bellyache who wants to bag a kudu that's bigger than all the others. Charles got the best buffalo, the best waterbuck, and the best lion. *I'm* going to get the best kudu."

He tossed town the whiskey.

*   *   *

By noon the next day the hunting party had assembled at a salt lick, a small clearing with many trails leading to it from the trees. Crouching carefully behind a blind made of branches and trees, Ernest and M'Cola peered through one of the holes in the crude wickerwork. There was no sign of game.

Ernest moved away into the brush and reappeared a moment later, buttoning his pants. M'Cola looked at him questioningly. Ernest grinned, though it was apparent that he didn't feel well. M'Cola passed him the water bottle. Ernest drank, then returned to his observation spot. The two men crouched together, making no sound.

M'Cola grabbed his arm, put a finger to his lips. There came a loud crack from the thicket, but then there was another noise, the sound of a motor, a car engine, down in the plain. Holding his breath, M'Cola pointed to the edge of the clearing.

"Kudu."

A large gray animal with white stripes on its flanks emerged from the brush. Huge antlers twisted forward, the large ears turned, twitching restlessly. From the plain the sounds of a motor were coming closer.

"*Piga, Bwana, doumi,*" whispered M'Cola.

Ernest carefully raised his rifle. Supporting himself on one knee, he took aim. The rifle barrel trembled. Beads of sweat appeared on Ernest's forehead. Sweat ran down into his eyes. He lowered the rifle to wipe them.

Suddenly the sound of the motor turned into a series of loud explosions, backfires that barked like guns. With one giant leap the buck disappeared into the thicket. M'Cola got up immediately.

"All over, *Bwana,*" he said.

Furious, Hemingway motioned to M'Cola to duck down again.

"No good, *Bwana. Hapana m'uzuri.*"

Miserable with disappointment, Ernest pounded his fist into the earth. M'Cola helped him to his feet and they set out along a sandy path in the direction of the motor, a few hundred yards away. Ernest had to stop several times, gripping his stomach and drinking from the canteen. M'Cola looked at him anxiously.

"Africa smells good," said Hemingway.

In a ditch along the path was a truck. Leaning over the vehicle's open hood was a robust, bowlegged man. He introduced himself to Hemingway. His name was Koritschoner, an Austrian.

"Sounds like you've got ignition trouble," said Hemingway. "If you want to come along, we've got a mechanic back at camp."

Koritschoner thanked him, asking his name.

"Hemingway?" asked the Austrian. "Now, that sounds familiar. Any relation to Ernest Hemingway, the poet?"

Ernest beamed. "You know his work?"

"Of course. I've read him in *Querschnitt*."

"Ah," said Ernest. "A German magazine I've written a few dirty poems for. Yes, I'm Ernest Hemingway."

Both men laughed, shook hands.

"What are you doing here?" Koritschoner asked.

"Hunting."

"Not ivory, I hope."

"Kudus," said Ernest.

Koritschoner was skeptical. "You, an intelligent man, a poet—killing kudus?"

"And I'd have got one if it hadn't been for your damned truck," said Hemingway. Suddenly he was wracked by cramps. He went into the undergrowth, reappearing a moment later. His face was twisted with pain.

"You don't seem to be in very good shape," said the Austrian.

"It's been on and off for the past couple of weeks," said Ernest. M'Cola handed him the canteen and he drank greedily.

"You'd better do something about it," said the Austrian.

"Best to just ignore it."

Saying that, Ernest collapsed. M'Cola and Koritschoner carried him to the shade of a large tree. The Austrian looked at M'Cola. "Go back to camp," he ordered. "Get help. Bring blankets, and make sure there's plenty of water. I'll stay here till you get back. Now hurry!"

M'Cola looked at Ernest anxiously, then ran off.

Ernest lay on his back and looked up at the tree.

"Comes and goes," he said. "I'll be all right."

"I don't get it," said Koritschoner. "You're a writer, a sensitive person, and you go out flinging lead at lions and kudus. Do you hate animals?"

Hemingway shook his head from side to side.

"No. But I don't mind killing them, if I kill cleanly. Animals are there to be hunted."

"Who taught you that?"

"My father."

"You enjoy killing?"

Ernest smiled. "Most people don't know anything about the real joy of killing," he explained. "And death is one of the greatest subjects a man can write about. I know death. I write about what I know."

"And morality?"

"I don't know anything about that. All I know is it's moral if it feels good, immoral if it feels bad. There's nothing immoral about hunting because it makes me feel very good."

"So I see."

* * *

That night Ernest lay still on a cot under the mosquito net while Pauline swabbed his brow. He had a high fever and was shivering, trying not to give in to the fits of weakness, pain, and nausea that flowed over him in waves. The malady was obvious: malaria.

He looked up at Charles and Percival, who stood in the entrance to the tent. "Hello, Charles," he said politely. "I'll bet you got one. Did you?"

Nodding, Charles came forward.

It was difficult for Ernest to speak. "That's marvelous," he said. "You win again."

"There were three of them," said Charles. "All huge. I didn't know which was the biggest. They gave us hell."

"I'm terribly happy you got one," said Ernest. "Doubtless a prize specimen."

"A prize kudu."

Laboriously, Ernest propped himself up on one arm. His breath was strained, quick and shallow.

"I hunted hard," he said. "I swear to God. I almost had him. Damn the Austrian!"

"You'll get your kudu," Charles said. "A monster. But you've got to get well first."

Ernest slumped back, completely exhausted.

Outside the tent Percival, Charles and Koritschoner held a conference.

"He's running a high temperature," said the white hunter. "It's malaria. We've got to get him to a hospital. We'll need a plane."

"You should radio to Viktoria Nyanza," Koritschoner suggested. "Fatty Pearson's there with his two-seated Puss-Moth biplane."

A moment later Charles was on the radio.

* * *

Pauline dissolved two quinine tablets in a glass of water and tried to make her husband drink. But Ernest was delirious. He waved the glass away, shaking his head from side to side, his eyes closed.

"Not that stuff!" he ordered. "Bring me a whiskey and soda! And stop carrying on!"

Pauline dried his forehead.

"No! No, please, Dad . . . no."

Ernest could see everything clearly, though the scene was somewhat out of focus around the edges: A large, darkened room. Laid out in state in the middle of the room was his father, eyes closed, hands folded over his chest. The trousers were a bit too short so that the boots stuck out a little. Ernest's mother, dressed in mourning, stood before the corpse. She spoke slowly.

"Your father went to the cellar to burn some papers. When he came back up he said he'd like to rest for a while up in his room before dinner. He went up. And just a few minutes later we heard the shot."

Grace was holding the Smith & Wesson revolver in her hand.

"He did it with this," she said, giving it to him.

Then he heard another voice, his father's. But it

was from a different, much earlier time, when Ernest was a child.

"Son, always remember, only cowards commit suicide. Don't ever forget that, son. Only cowards."

Then everything went black.

* * *

He awoke, breathing with difficulty, shaken by another chill. Pauline sat next to him, holding his hand. Ernest looked at her severely.

"She's a bitch," he said.

"Who, dear?"

"Mother. She's extravagant and selfish. All she ever cared about was the big house, her conservatory, her standard of living. She undid him. She ruined him."

"Darling," said Pauline, applying a damp towel to his brow, "try not to talk. Just rest."

"She suffocated him! No way for him to escape! It's all her fault he killed himself."

Pauline ran her hand through his wet hair. "There now," she said, "it's all right. He shot himself. That's what hurts. You can't blame your mother for that."

He looked at her, wild-eyed. "It was hell for him! He couldn't take it anymore. That's just the way it was when Hadley wanted you and me to separate. We all had to suffer!"

Pauline began to cry. "Yes, dear, yes. Please . . . I love you. Try to sleep."

Ernest sank back into his pillow. His voice grew lower, harder to understand.

"He gave up. He should have fought. He should have pulled through . . ."

There was a silence, then his eyes opened. He spoke clearly, staring at the tent's ridgepole.

"He knew! My father knew what he was doing! *He knew!*"

* * *

At dawn the boys lit fires to mark the end of the provisional landing strip. Clouds of smoke billowed up into the blue early morning sky. Soon a biplane appeared. It slipped in at a slant, landed, and came to a bumpy stop. The boys carried Ernest out of the camp and to the airstrip on his cot. Too weak to climb into the plane himself, he was boosted by Percival and Charles. In his seat, he looked at Pauline, tried to smile. She took his hand.

"You're going to be fine," she said. "You're the champ!"

"When I get back," he said slowly, "we'll go out for kudus."

"Absolutely."

"You look good, Pauline. How do you feel?" he asked.

"Strong."

"Ah. Strong and sexy and smart as they come. We're the champs."

* * *

Aloft, Hemingway looked down. In the savanna, from all directions, were the trails of wild game which led to the watering hole where the camp was located. Herds of thousands of gnus, zebras, and antelopes were in the far distance. Then the Ngorongoro crater appeared, filled with green woods like a bowl of salad. Before them, high and white in the sun, was the flat peak of Kilimanjaro. Fatty Pearson pointed to it.

"Kilimanjaro. Highest mountain in Africa, almost six thousand meters. Go up there in the summer and you're as close as you can get to the sun without leaving the ground."

Ernest looked around, taking it all in.

"I'll always come back," he said. "I like the life here. Life is real here." He pointed to the mountain's peak. "Over there, the west peak? The Masai call it Ngaja Ngai, the House of God."

They looked at the peak, said nothing. Pearson thought Hemingway had fallen asleep, until he spoke. His voice was calm, his words well chosen, the words of a storyteller:

"They say someone found a skeleton of a leopard just below that peak. Parched, frozen, there was nothing to eat or hunt. No one knows what the leopard was doing up so high."

Key West, Florida—Fall, 1935

African trophies—the stuffed heads of rhinoceri, sable antelopes, waterbucks, kudus—were mounted on the walls throughout the house. Spears, bows, arrows, and shields stood in corners, hung from the ceilings. Framed photographs of Ernest and Pauline in their bush garb, holding rifles and standing behind dead animals, were everywhere.

In the middle of the spacious dining room there was a large, thin wooden crate, opened and empty, its packing wool cluttering the floor. Ernest, at the top of a ladder, was hanging a large oil painting when Pauline and Ernest's new friend, the writer John Dos Passos, walked in.

"Looks familiar," said Dos Passos, looking at the painting.

"Should be," said Hemingway. "It's Miro's *The Farm*."

"Well, it's certainly better than that kudu head of yours that stares at us so reproachfully," said Pauline. "I remember it from Paris."

Ernest came down the ladder and studied the painting. "Hadley lent it out to some exhibition in Chicago. I just happened to read about it in the paper. I gave her a call and she agreed to entrust it to me for five years. Nice of her. I can still remember giving it to her for her birthday."

"How is Hadley?" asked Dos Passos. "Are you still in touch?"

"She's happily remarried. Her husband is managing editor of the *Chicago Daily News*," said Pauline.

For a moment Ernest was silent, lost in thought. "Paris was a good place to be young," he said. "But now it's no good. It's full of emigrants trying to get away from the Nazis, and full of Nazis spying on them. And everybody's talking about the next war as if invitations had already been sent out."

He gave Dos Passos a slap on the back, then turned to Pauline. "Time to go fishing!" he announced. "Why not come along, Pauline?"

"What about the children?"

"They'll be all right without you. Come."

Pauline shook her head, looking sad. "I can't," she said. "I don't want to."

"We won't be back till tomorrow night," said her husband.

Now she was angry. "Ernest, you know very well I can't go. I have lots of responsibilities here."

"And I don't?" Ernest was defensive.

"As a fisherman or a writer?" Pauline flung back.

"We'd have no trouble living off the catch," he said.

"Ha!"

Ernest went outside. Crossing the wide veranda he walked down into the courtyard where their boys came running to him. He scooped them up, one on either arm.

"Take us with you, Pop!" they squealed.

Smiling, their father shook his head. "Someone has to stay here and protect your great old mamma," he said. "I'd be worried if you boys weren't around here when I'm gone."

Pauline and Dos Passos came up slowly, talking between themselves. "It's hard, John," she said. "Since Ernest got his boat I hardly ever see him. He's out there day and night. Sometimes I think he doesn't need me—want me—anymore."

"And what about you?" asked the writer.

"I manage. I've got the children, the house . . ."

Ernest shouted at them from the car. "Hey, Pfife! Don't make such a face. I'd be lost without you and the boys. Sure you won't come?"

"I'm sure."

Dos Passos joined Hemingway in the car. They both wore soiled fishing clothes, baggy pants and bloody sweatshirts, sneakers and long-billed hats.

"See you tomorrow night!" Ernest waved.

* * *

Doing better than sixteen knots, the *Pilar,* a very modern sportfisherman, plowed through the dark blue, almost violet water of the Gulf Stream. Ernest stood on the flying bridge, hands on the wheel, looking out over the sea with a look of excitement and concentration. Beside him his hired captain, Carlos Gutiérrez, scanned the horizon for fish. Dos Passos was strapped into the fighting chair in the cockpit, ready for the first strike. Holding the largest rod and reel aboard, he let out line.

"What do you think, Dos?" shouted Ernest. "Seventy-five horsepower! Sixteen knots at full throttle . . . plenty of room."

"Must have cost a bundle!"

"Ha! I made a down payment with the royalties of *Winner Take Nothing* and a couple of short stories. It was my gift to me! She's a great little fishing machine, eh? Named her after Pauline. I used to call her Pilar . . . a long time ago."

A formation of flying fish leaped from the water

and sailed over the surface in wide black waves. The bait, trolled behind the stern, hopped over the swells. Suddenly Ernest let out a yell.

"Over there!" He poined to a patch of water on the port side. "See him?"

The sickle-shaped fin of a big marlin surfaced, wiggling just past the *Pilar*. Ernest handed the helm over to Carlos and climbed down into the cockpit. The fish was nearing the bait.

"Let him take it, John, let him take it."

The bait disappeared.

"Good, good!" He slapped Dos Passos's back. "Now jam it and hit him! Give it to him!"

Dos Passos released the star drag and the line began to zing out. The marlin turned and dived.

"Hit him, hit him!"

Screwing down the drag, Dos Passos braced himself against the footrest, a death-grip on the rod. The reel began to whine like a mill saw as the marlin broke the surface in a long, perpendicular jump. For an instant it was almost motionless, striped lavender-blue in the sun; then it fell back into the water, throwing up a mountain of spray.

Hemingway had plenty of advice: "The hook's set! See it, Dos? Up in the corner of his jaw. Okay, Carlos, let's go! Open her up!"

Throwing the engine into reverse, Carlos backed the boat down on the fish as fast as it would go. A wall of water flew up and was blown over the transom, soaking both fishermen.

"Jesus Maria!" shouted the Cuban captain. "He's going hard and not stopping!"

"He's diving!" shouted Dos Passos.

"He won't be able to go too deep," said Ernest knowingly. "He got too much air when he jumped."

"He jumped like a race horse!"

The tackle ripped at Dos Passos's shoulders. The

inch-thick laminated bamboo rod leaped from side to side in his arms.

"Now bring him up!"

Dos Passos labored to bring in the line. Suddenly, up on the bridge, Carlos stamped his foot. He pointed out to the open sea.

"Bad company! Sharks! A whole school!"

Ernest saw them. He looked at Dos Passos. "Hold him! Can you hold him?"

Dos Passos nodded. Winding the big Penn Senator 16.0 reel, he cranked in a few more yards of braided linen. Curious, the sharks came closer.

Furious, Hemingway ran below. He emerged a moment later, carrying a Thompson submachine gun wrapped in an oil-soaked sheepskin. He pulled back the bolt, inserted the spring-wound ammunition drum, and climbed to the flying bridge. As the sharks came closer he took aim and fired.

The staccato burst filled the air. The water foamed bloodred. Ernest squeezed the trigger again and again.

"Ernie!" Dos Passos shouted. "What the hell are you doing?"

Ignoring him, Ernest emptied the drum, inserted another, and fired until the last round.

* * *

It was dusk when they reached the harbor dock. Children were playing and many tourists were there to watch the sunset and check the day's fishing catch. Ernest and John were completely smeared with fish blood and salt. Using blocks, they pulled from the water the piteous remains of the marlin, twelve feet long before the sharks got to it. Now, all that was left was the head, large as a horse's. A brightly clothed tourist moved closer with his wife. He saw the fish, laughed, and took a picture with a Brownie box camera.

"Looks like Fatso down there didn't have much luck," he said to his wife, loud enough for Ernest to hear. A few curious onlookers laughed.

Hemingway appeared, his face contorted in rage. "You call me 'Fatso'?" he demanded.

"Oh my God, Harold," said the tourist's wife. "That's Ernest Hemingway!"

Ernest stepped over the gunnel and onto the dock, facing the tourist squarely.

"Well, excuse me, Mr Hemingway."

"You call me 'Fatso'?"

"I was referring to the fish," he said lamely. Then, "We both love your books, Mr.—"

Ernest looked at the crowd that had collected. "Who wants to take on Fatso?" he shouted. "I'll fight anybody!"

Dos Passos, who had been drinking whiskey with Hemingway all the way home, tried to calm his friend. "Ernie, let's go, huh? Time for dinner, Pauline, the kids."

"Who'll fight me? What's the matter, no *cajones?* Come on, black or white, I don't care! Two hundred and fifty dollars for anybody who can go three rounds with me!"

No one moved. Dos Passos took his arm and dragged him away, toward the row of waiting harbor bars.

"Ernie, what you need is a shot," he said. Hemingway liked the idea.

* * *

It was hot in the bar, packed with locals and tourists, guests spilling onto the sidewalk. The counter was three-men deep with men in dungarees, some without hats, some with straws, others with old military caps and steel helmets. The jukebox was blaring "Isla Capri" and almost everyone was drunk.

Standing at the back end of the counter, Ernest

and John took in the view while tossing down shots of white rum and chasing them with gulps of beer.

Their attention was drawn to an aging drunk, a man in a shabby army uniform, on crutches and with a broken leg, standing on top of the billiard table. He was having fun calling guests over and then hitting them with his crutches. He saw Ernest.

"Hey, Papa!" he shouted hoarsely. "Hey, everybody! There's the champ! Papa Hemingway, the champ! Hey Papa, come here! I accept your challenge, $250! Okay?"

Ernest laughed. "So you can bash me over the head with your crutches?" He gestured to Skinner, the black bartender. "Give that man a drink."

There was a commotion across the room. A man at the counter was pulled back by two others. One of them punched him in the face, the other in the ribs.

"Give it to the bastard!" someone shouted. "Sock him in the mouth!" yelled another.

Struck squarely in the jaw, the man fell forward onto his knees.

"That was a hell of a punch," said Ernest admiringly.

A man stuck his face in Ernest's. "The rat bastard comes to town and deposits all his pay in the bank," he said, slurring his words. "Then he hangs around leeching off everybody else. When I hit him just now his jaw felt like a bag of marbles!"

A small crowd formed around Ernest and John. Hemingway treated them to a round of drinks.

"Great fellows," he said to Dos Passos.

"Who are they?"

"War veterans. They live in the work camps on the Upper and Lower Matecumbe Keys. Building streets and bridges for the government. Miami to Key West, plenty of work for everybody. Fifteen dollars a month, Dos. Slave wages. Today's payday, the poor saps."

"Any Communists in the camp?" asked Dos Passos, whose political writings were, at the time, strongly from the Left.

"About forty out of two thousand," said Ernest.

A veteran spoke up. "Takes too much discipline to be a Communist," he said logically. "It's not easy for a drunk to get involved. See, our government shipped us down here to get rid of us. We're an embarrassment. They don't just want us out of sight. They want us off the earth! At camp they did everything they could so an epidemic would break out, but it didn't work. The poor bastards just don't want to croak."

Just then a big, broad-shouldered black man approached Ernest. He stood a head taller than all the rest, and seemed sober.

"Mr. Ernest," he said quietly. "You know me, sir. Willard."

"Yes, Willard?"

"Mr. Ernest, I'd like to try it with you for the two-fifty."

Hemingway smiled. "Okay, Willard. Tomorrow morning, before we go out fishing."

The black man grinned, just slightly. "No, sir, Mr. Ernest. I'd like to try it out with you right here and right now."

Ernest nodded, a spark in his eye. "Okay, I'll just go get the gloves."

"No, sir," said Willard. "I'd like to try it out with you right here and right now without gloves."

"Fine," said Ernest.

The guests cheered, everyone started shouting. Quickly they formed a square about the size of a boxing ring. Ernest and Willard, stripped to the waist, squared off. Then they went at it. Willard was big, huge, but Hemingway was the better pugilist. Suddenly he landed a hard right hook and Willard went down. Joe Russel, owner of the bar, rang a bell. He counted Willard out, then rang the bell again.

"The winner!" he shouted, raising Ernest's hand.

"By a knockout, Ernest Hemingway. And to cele-brate—a round of drinks, Skinner! On the house!"

* * *

The sun was rising as Ernest and John left the bar. They walked down Grand Street. It had rained earlier and the street was wet and muddy.

"How's the hand?" asked Dos Passos.

"A little swollen."

Dos Passos sighed. "Well, brawling's always nasty."

"Once you've started," said Ernest, "you have to win."

"I guess so. Did you enjoy yourself?"

Hemingway stopped, faced his friend, smiled. "I made a damn fool of myself, didn't I? Go on, say it."

"You've said it yourself, Ernie."

A milkman was delivering bottles of milk when they came up to Dos Passos's hotel, the Atlantis. They sat on the wooden steps and looked out at the muddy street.

"Hell," said Hemingway, "I'm getting tired of being Key West's number-one attraction. Everybody slaps me on the shoulder like we're old buddies."

"What about the veterans, Ernie?" Dos Passos asked. "They trust you. Why not help them?"

"How?"

"Write about them. Write about what's happening to them in these glorious United States."

"Boring."

"Boring? The worker's struggle, the miserable liv-ing conditions, the endless lines at public kitchens? You call that boring?"

Ernest shook his head. "That's material for the committed social critic, John Dos Passos. Not my cup of tea."

"Sure. But bullfights, hunting lions, fishing . . ."

"At least it's true. I write about what I've experienced. I'm the only one in this godforsaken country who can do it."

Dos Passos was deadly serious. "Toying with death," he said, "is the only thing that fascinates you. War, maybe, too. Why not the reasons for war, why not the people who profit from it?"

Hemingway dismissed the idea with a gesture. "John, the hardest thing in the world is to write honest prose. Whoever chooses politics is lying. Left or right, there's none of that in writing. There's only good and bad. Liberals, conservatives—I'd like to take a machine gun and mow down the whole lot."

"Like the sharks?"

Ernest shook his head sullenly. "Spare me the sermon," he said.

* * *

The large dining room table was set for three people. Wine and champagne were on the table, in coolers. The first rays of the rising sun were reflected in the crystal glasses. Pauline, still dressed, was asleep on the couch. The noise from Ernest's typewriter woke her. Dazed, she needed a moment to orient herself.

Ernest was at his standing desk, a bureau in his bedroom. With two fingers he slowly pecked a handwritten manuscript into the typewriter. Beside it was his cat which he occasionally stroked. Pauline appeared at the door. Ernest didn't notice her till she spoke.

"I waited up for you with dinner."

Ernest looked away from his work, smiled. He put the cat down gently on the floor.

"Sorry, Pfife," he said. "Did I wake you? Why aren't you in bed?"

"Where's Dos?"

"I took him back to his hotel."

"Are you hungry? Want something to eat?"

He shook his head. As he looked at her, he realized she had dyed her hair to a reddish brown.

"What did you do to your hair?"

"Do you like it?" She touched her hair.

"No."

Pauline showed her disappointment. She was almost embarrassed. "I thought you'd like it," she said.

He shrugged.

Looking down, she spoke quietly. "Things are so
different now. We used to be . . . one person. You used
my bathroom, you drank whiskey from my toothbrush
glass . . ." She looked up at him, tears in her eyes.
"You used to sleep in my bed."

He said nothing, stared at her.

She looked away. "I miss you so much when
you're out in your boat. It hurts. It's just the way it hurt
when Hadley made us separate. That's how I feel now."

She began to cry. He put his arm around her.

"I miss you, too, sometimes," he said weakly.
"Look, I don't go fishing to hurt you. I feel good when
I'm on the *Pilar*. I'm excited—the way I feel when I'm
working. And I feel good when I'm with you. I love
you, Pfife, you and the boys."

He kissed her, whispered something in her ear.
She smiled and took him by the hand.

"We have to be careful. You know what the doctor
said."

He kissed her on the mouth, cutting her off. "It's
all right, daughter," he whispered. "Hey, I'm really
happy here, happiest I've ever been."

A few days later Ernest was standing at the typewriter in his room, patiently writing and rewriting a
single page. Occasionally he looked at the barometer,
which was well below storm level and falling rapidly.
He went to the window and looked outside. Everything
was calm.

An hour later the storm erupted, first with a high,

dry wind, then rain. Ernest bolted the shutters, closed the windows, then went downstairs where Pauline was struggling with the big veranda shutters. They worked together without speaking, then went into the living room to wait. Ernest turned on the radio. A hurricane, the largest of the season, was well on its way and Key West was directly in its path.

Outside, the wind howled through the streets, sweeping paper, twigs, leaves, dust, and dirt high into the air. The tall palms bent and shook. Flying from the Coast Guard station's flagpole was a large red flag with a black square in the middle—hurricane. Waves washed over the promenade along the beach, splashing onto the street.

In the house the noise was almost deafening. Pauline and the children sat at the dining room table playing cards. They tried to be at ease, but it was a pretense. Everyone could hear what was going on outside, the sound of trees crashing, windows breaking. Ernest sat by the radio, waiting for each fifteen-minute report.

"The *Pilar*'s battened down," he said. "Double canvas, double lines."

"Don't worry," said Pauline. "It'll be safe in the old submarine harbor."

"Unless the wind shifts to the southwest. I've got two anchors down, but it's still not enough. She'll be washed up on the jetty. Hell, I haven't even paid her off yet."

She went over and put her arms around him. "Nothing to do now but wait," she said.

Ernest and his family were all asleep on the couch when the radio blared an announcement, waking them.

"The hurricane has passed over the Florida Keys, headed north and out to sea. The fishing village in Long Key was completely destroyed."

Ernest rubbed his eyes, turned up the volume.

"Hardest hit were the veterans camps on the Upper and Lower Matecumbe Keys, where the hurricane left hundreds dead. The Coast Guard is urgently requesting volunteers with boats to help locate and bring back the bodies."

"Before the sharks get to them," said Ernest. He got up and left the room.

* * *

The *Pilar* cut smoothly through the water past mangrove islands. Corpses floated in the shallows, washed ashore on the incoming tide. Ernest and Carlos watched a shark circle their boat as they labored to drag a body on board. Carlos smacked the surface of the water with an oar. The shark moved off. Looking down, Ernest recognized one of the corpses—the man with the broken leg and crutches he'd seen at the waterfront bar. He turned away.

* * *

Max Perkins was on the phone from his office at Scribner's, in New York.

"Ernie, I'm reading your hurricane story on the front page of the *New Masses*. Why in the world did you choose that paper? You could have written about the hurricane for anyone."

Ernest was at his desk in the living room in Key West. He replied carefully and honestly.

"Because the *New Masses* telegraphed and asked me to write it for them. I said okay, 2,800 words without renumeration."

"You wrote it for nothing?"

"I don't want to make money on anybody's death, Max."

"All right. And the charges you make against the government? You're sticking to them?"

"The hurricane warning came Saturday night, Max. They had all Sunday and Monday to evacuate the veterans. And why didn't they? Because the government wanted to get rid of them. That's why they were sent here, to be forgotten, to die. They fought for their country in the worst war ever, and then their country took care of them. It worked out beautifully, didn't it?"

"Ernie, the *New Masses* is a leftest newspaper. Are you over on the left now?"

Ernest exploded. "The hell with your left! Max, when you came down here—do you remember the nice girl a few miles from the ferry who ran the sandwich shop? She was a daughter of one of the veterans, she was down here to be with him. He's gone now, feeding the sharks. She ended up in the mangroves, bloated, stinking, her breasts blown up big as balloons, flies between her legs. What's that got to do with the left? Explain it to me. Marx and Engels, they never wrote about that!"

"Well, you might be right," said the editor. "But I think I'd better come down for a few days. We should talk about this."

Two days later Ernest and Max took a walk down Southard Street to its intersection with Duval. A truck came toward them, then turned in at a small courtyard. Day laborers jumped down from the back of the truck and lined up in front of a doorway to collect their pay. On Duval Street a large group of people had lined up in front of the cinema, waiting for tickets. Ernest noted the contrast, those who have and those who have not.

"The Fascists are getting ready for war in Europe," he said. "It could happen any day now, like a long-planned murder. Spain's just the prelude. Franco against the Republic."

Max Perkins turned to his favorite writer. "Ernie, so many authors are going to Spain. It's my worst nightmare that you'll all be killed. You're not a newspaper reporter, you're a writer. I thought you didn't care about politics."

"It's not a matter of politics," Ernest replied

strongly. "It's a matter of justice and injustice, that's all. Any writer who's lost his feeling for that should stop writing."

"You have friends in Spain, eh? On both sides?" Max asked.

"I've always been on the republican side of anything. Makes no difference if it's the Spanish or the American civil war. We're talking about justice, Max."

At the front steps to a waterfront bar stood a woman. Martha Gellhorn appeared undecided, peering inside the saloon as Ernest entered. Martha recognized the famous author and his editor, but said nothing as she waited on the stairs.

The bar was half full, a few sailors and locals hanging around, some Cubans and loose women in the booths, talking, laughing, drinking, and playing cards. Ernest wore crumpled khaki shorts and a fish blood–smeared T-shirt, Perkins was dressed as if for the office in a double-breasted suit with an elegant tie. Skinner poured the drinks.

Perkins was deadly serious. "You're going to the front?"

"That's the plan."

"You're going to fight?"

"No. I'm going to write. The *North American New Alliance* wants me to report on the Spanish Civil War."

Perkins took a sip from his drink and considered his words carefully before he spoke. "And what about the new novel you've started? *To Have and Have Not*. Are you just going to drop it?"

Ernest shrugged guiltily.

Perkins continued. "After all, Ernie, it's possible you may not come back. You want to leave a book half finished? A writer should always write as though he were going to die when he gets to the end. I believe *you* said that."

Ernest quickly downed a shot of rum. "Okay," he agreed. "I'll finish it. If you'll give me a $4,000 advance."

Max almost choked on his whiskey.

"As a loan," Ernest added.

"What do you need so much money for?"

"Medical supplies. For the Republican troops."

Just then Martha Gellhorn made up her mind to enter the bar. For a moment all conversation died down as everyone looked at the elegant newcomer who came through the doorway. Martha, tall, slim, blond, strode confidently across the room to a free table. She sat down, seemingly oblivious of the admiring stares. Ernest stared at her. Martha, looking around challengingly, beckoned to the bartender.

Skinner grinned broadly from ear to ear. He raised his eyebrows.

"Oh, man," he said to Ernest. "Ain't this joint getting elegant?"

Max stared at Martha reflectively. He looked away from her a moment, then he shook his head. "I know that blond," he said.

Ernest looked at him, incredulous. "Max, you never cease to amaze me."

"I know her professionally. Name's Martha Gellhorn. Very promising writer. Wrote a book about the plight of the unemployed. Big success. I can't think of the title."

Perkins wrinkled his forehead, running titles through his memory trying to remember.

Ernest Hemingway was one of those large men who can move very quickly when they want to. In a flash he took up the tray on which Skinner had put the Gellhorn order, walked over to her table, and served the drink.

"Madam," he said with a deep bow, "this is on me, if you'll permit me the pleasure."

Amazed, Martha stared at him. Ernest became increasingly nervous. He began to falter.

"Unless you'd rather not . . ."

Martha Gellhorn looked down. "But of course," she said. "I'd be delighted, Mr. Hemingway."

A big grin spread across Ernest's face as he sat down with them. Perkins, who had watched the whole scene from the bar, picked up his drink and joined them. Ernest carried most of the conversation, all of it about Spain, the civil war and injustice. He never took his eyes off her.

* * *

Later. It was dark outside when Pauline walked down Duval Street and peeked into the bar. She couldn't see much. Entering the bar, she walked over to the counter. The place had filled up and was very noisy now. When Skinner spotted her he pointed to the table in the corner.

"Over there, Mrs. Hemingway." He winked. "The beauty and the beast."

Pauline made her way through the boisterous crowd, then stopped behind Max and Ernest, who had their backs turned to her. She could see Martha plainly at her table and could hear the conversation.

"Your first novel, Miss Gellhorn," said Max. "The title—*What Mad Pursuit*—is taken from Keats, eh?"

"Yes."

"I'm sorry to say I haven't read your stories yet," Ernest said.

Perkins spoke up. "You made quite an impact with *The Troubles I've Seen*, Miss Gellhorn. I liked it very much."

Martha interrupted: "The National Relief Agency asked me to investigate conditions among unemployed workers in the South. I went there and I wrote, but nobody read my reports. So I quit reporting and tried to put my experiences into a few great stories instead."

Ernest touched her hand briefly. "That's the only way to do it if you want to write the good stuff," he said. "What are you working on now?"

Pauline was staring candidly at Martha. Martha sensed the looks and grew more and more insecure. But she continued the conversation.

"I'm working on a new novel, set in Germany. It deals with the Nazis' rise to power. I was there. It's terrible. Innocent people being beat up in the streets, fear everywhere. I'm going back in a few months."

"You're not afraid?" Ernest inquired, wondering how she would answer.

"I beg your pardon?" was all she said.

Ernest nodded. "What do you think of the Nazis?"

Just then he noticed Martha looking behind him.

Turning around, he was surprised to see Pauline standing there.

"Pauline dear," he said, neglecting to stand. "What a charming surprise."

Pauline's voice was frigid. "I've been waiting for you."

"Ah, yes," said Hemingway. He looked at Martha. "Martha Gellhorn, I'd like you to meet my wife, Pauline."

* * *

At the end of that week, when splendid weather had returned, the Hemingways went to the beach. With Martha Gellhorn. Pauline sat under a huge umbrella, reading *Vogue*. The children, with their nanny, were building a sand castle nearby. Pauline looked up from her magazine frequently, staring at the water.

Ernest and Martha were swimming. They dived into the lakelike sea. After a few minutes they ran to the towels they'd left by the water's edge and dried themselves.

"Dos Passos and I are going to work on a documentary film together," said Ernest. "It's something being done about the civil war in Spain. We want to let Americans know what's going on, shake them up, show them how desperate the people in Spain really are."

"Sounds wonderful," Martha commented.

"Franco's waging a completely new kind of war against the Spanish people. A total war. It's the prelude to a much bigger war that none of us will be able to escape."

Martha shook her head sadly. "Everything's different in wartime. So intense, extreme. Working day and night. But living, too, swimming and feeling the sun in your hair and getting to know so many people. And everything all at once, because each day gets shorter and shorter. War changes everything."

"Sure," said Ernest, "but war can be exciting too. It offers the writer so much material. It speeds things up, brings out things in people you'd normally have to wait a lifetime for. But it's still the worst thing people can do to each other, the very worst."

"I know," said Martha. "But I'm going to Spain to fight the Fascists just the same. *All* writers are obligated to take a political stand."

Ernest looked at Martha. He spoke very slowly, an ironic undertone in his voice.

"A writer can make a good living from committing himself to a political cause. If he's on the winning side he's made. He becomes an ambassador, or maybe the government publishes a million copies of his book," he said.

Startled, Martha stared at Ernest, who shook his head. His expression changed. He stared out at the flat sea and spoke as though someone were exerting pressure on him.

"The hardest thing in the world, Martha, is writing good prose about people. Books should deal with people you love or hate, but not with people you have to study first."

He put his hand on her arm, continued.

"That's why you should only write about what you understand. What you know from firsthand experience. Write the truth wherever you find it. Whoever chooses politics as a way out is faking."

Pauline got up. She looked over at Ernest and Martha, waved them over. They ran up. Martha sat down on her towel, stretching her long legs. Ernest dropped into the sand next to the children. He looked at Pauline.

"Martha's going to stay here another few days," he said evenly.

Pauline forced herself to smile at Martha and Ernest. Her smile was forced, cold and masklike.

"How nice."

* * *

One week later Ernest stood on the balcony, looking at the Key West lighthouse flashing in the night. The giant beam wandered over the lawn, over the house and balcony. Looking through the picture window, he saw Pauline lying on a large double bed, the head of which was the carved door of a seventeenth-century Spanish cloister. There was a light sea breeze. Ernest went inside and lay down next to Pauline. She sat up.

"I'd so like to go to Spain with you," she said, pleading.

"That's not possible."

"Why not? I'm your wife."

"We've been through this, Pfife."

"Let's go through it again."

"You can't come to Spain because Spain is at war. A horrible war, much too dangerous for a woman. The boys need you and besides, I'll be working the whole time. You'd never even see me."

Pauline paused; then, "And Martha?"

"What Martha does is her own business," he snapped. "She's her own boss. There's a war to be covered."

"How come Martha can go and I can't?"

"Because she's a writer and she doesn't have children. Don't be stupid."

"I'm not stupid," said Pauline. "I'm your clever, witty wife. You used to talk to me about your work. You read me what you'd written. I typed your manuscripts, remember? We used to joke, make fun of people, laugh at the world. We used to make love, Ernest. But now, I don't even know what you're thinking anymore. It's like I don't know you, like I never did. Sometimes I think you've forgotten I'm even here."

He took her hand. "I've never treated you badly," he said lamely.

"No," she said. "You've never treated me badly. But there's no love between us anymore."

Pauline got up and went to the window. Ernest watched her silently. She turned around, her eyes welling with tears. She wiped them with the back of her hand, trembling.

"Very well. I'll be brave. I'll stay here and keep up appearances. I'll pretend to be busy and cheerful. But I'll really just be counting the days until you get back and my life here will finally start again."

She went back to the bed and sat down.

"You know, Ernest, when I was little my parents couldn't leave me alone for a second without my climbing up on some chair and falling off. Looks like nothing has really changed. I'm afraid of this war in Spain."

He took her hand. "I'll be careful, Pfife," he said. "I promise. Nothing's going to happen to me."

Pauline turned around. She laughed.

"That's not what I mean. What I'm afraid of isn't

bombs and bullets. What I fear is blond and young, with slim hips."

Ernest sighed.

Spain—Spring, 1937

From the battered, blown-out window of what was once a stately Spanish manor, Ernest watched the Republican troops start off through a small pine wood to attack the Fascist positions. The battle sounds grew louder, rifle and light machine-gun fire along with the explosions from heavy artillery and grenades.

Hemingway, Dos Passos, the film director, and a camera operator hunched on the floor, as they had been all morning and most of the afternoon. Freno, the camera operator, adjusted his telephoto lens and set it in a narrow crack in the manor's masonry.

"From this distance the tanks look like little toys," he said softly.

"The People's Army on the offensive!" said Dos Passos.

Ernest was cynical. "Offensive? Any idiot can see this attack's a total washout."

Suddenly there came the whistling sounds of gunshots all around them. The men ducked and took cover while bullets riddled the opposite wall and ricocheted across the room with ugly zinging sounds. Glass shattered, Ernest cursed.

"*La puta que los pario!*" he snarled. "Moroccan sharpshooters. Get away from the window. Watch the camera."

"My ass!" shouted the director. "Keep shooting," he ordered.

Freno looked through the lens. "Three tanks! Come on, make it snappy."

A new round of fire poured through the window,

ripping into the plaster ceiling. The men were calm.

"Got enough film?"

"All out, dammit. Gimme a new spool!"

While the director and Freno changed the spool, Ernest low-crawled across the room to the balcony door. He ducked as bullets tore over his head. During a pause he gathered up a few ripped planks and a piece of awning. Hugging them to him he crawled back across the room to where the camera was positioned. Using the planks and shredded canvas, he and Dos Passos built a sort of blind for the camera's long lens.

The director looked through the aperture. "Get the planks out of the frame," he said.

Freno shook his head. "No, leave them. They get rid of the glare."

The operator let the camera roll. Ernest pointed in the direction of the Fascist positions.

"They're crazy about lens reflections," he said. "From over there they think they've spotted binoculars, and where there are binoculars there's often a command post full of officers."

The director looked up. He and the others were covered by a thick layer of white dust. He spat plaster from his mouth.

Okay, I think we've got enough. Let's pack it up."

"Wonderful," said the camera operator. "Now I can spend the whole night cleaning this damn thing again. Movies!"

Crouching low, the men left their observation post. They carried the camera and tripod carefully down the destroyed staircase. They treated the equipment as if it were human, a friend who could not walk.

Behind the manor house were a few low clay farmhouses. The farmers were loading their few possessions onto a truck; mattresses, furniture, pots and pans. Some herded animals from a stall, others simply sat in stunned silence. An old man sat on the ground, propped up by a stone wall. His body trembling, he watched the procession of refugees pass by him. When Hemingway saw him he stopped.

"Where do you come from?" he asked in Spanish.

The old man pointed in the direction from where the refugees were coming. "I was taking care of the animals. But I had to leave them behind. Two goats, a cat, and four pairs of pigeons. The captain ordered me to go, because of the artillery."

"You have no family?"

"No, just the animals. The cat will be all right. Nothing will happen to the cat. A cat can take care of itself. But what will become of the others?"

Ernest beckoned to the film crew. Then he looked down at the old man, sitting there on the side of the road, tired, expressionless.

"The pigeons will fly away," he said kindly.

"Yes, they will fly away. But the goats? What about the goats? I was taking care of the animals. I was just taking care of the animals . . ."

Freno set up the camera. Dos Passos looked at Hemingway, then at the old man. "What's wrong with him?"

"He was taking care of the animals," said Ernest. "Two goats, a cat, and four pairs of pigeons. He had to leave them. Now he doesn't want to go."

Freno focused, the camera rolled.

"You must go from here," Ernest said gently.

"Where are the trucks going?" the old man asked.

Ernest pointed down the road.

"I know nobody in that direction."

Ernest signaled to Freno, who turned off the camera. "The whole world has abandoned these people," he said. "Everyone just talked and paid promises. The meanest, lowest way to end this thing. You can't win a war with empty promises."

They left the old man, still sitting, watching.

* * *

Sandbags were stacked shoulder-high in front of the glass revolving door leading to the reception hall of the Hotel Florida, in Madrid. There was plenty of activity in the hall. Foreign journalists stood around in small groups, talking. Some of them had set up typewriters and were in the process of writing stories. As always, the switchboard operator was besieged with incoming and outgoing long-distance calls.

Ernest sat in a chair in the barbershop, waiting for a shave. Beside him sat an excessively heavy man whose face was completely lathered. He held a glass with a thick yellow liquid in it. Ernest recognized him.

"Howdy, Tom."

The fat man sat up a bit. "Why, hello, Hem," he said. "How'd it go today?" It was Delmer, of the *Daily Mail*.

"Lousy," said Ernest. "We'll try again tomorrow. The Fascists have dug in everywhere. Done a damn good job. We don't have enough firepower to make sure they'll stay put, and we don't have any heavy artillery to blast them out."

"We took the new speedway," said Delmer. "We pushed as far as the corridor leading to the university quarter. I heard that Duran lost more than half his brigade."

"What are you drinking?"

Delmer reached down and produced a bottle of wine. "Help yourself, Hem," he said, handing him the bottle. "I finagled it."

Ernest read the label. "Chateau d'Yquem, 1909."

"Paid six cents a bottle. Got a dozen."

"Where?"

"From the king's wine cellar."

Ernest poured the sweet, heavy wine into a little glass from the barber's shelf. He raised it to Delmer.

"Well, then. To the king, Alfonso XIII," he toasted.

He spat out the wine. Making a face, Ernest got up

and walked through the reception hall to the bar, which was crowded with men in uniform, civilians, reporters and whores.

"Whiskey," he said to the bartender. "Double double."

He had to elbow a bit to get the glass to his mouth. Then, as he was taking a long drink, someone bumped into him, causing some of the whiskey to spill. Ernest whirled around furiously. Behind him was a tall, thin man wearing a smeared and greasy leather jacket with insignias indicating he was an officer in the foreign volunteer force, the Lincoln Battalion. His face was black with soot and there were dark rings under his eyes. Ernest clapped him on the back.

"Bob, where've you been?" he inquired.

"Casa de Campo. I left my tank there. We're done for the day." The young man raised his glass to his mouth. His hand was trembling. It was covered with oil, and the space between his thumb and index finger was black from gunpowder. He held out his other hand, which was also trembling.

"I was there," said Ernest. "We filmed your attack."

"How'd you like it?"

Ernest shook his head. "Not at all."

Bob agreed. "Me neither. Why the hell do we have to attack positions like that head-on? We're going to try it again tomorrow. It'll be murder."

"When's it going to start? Just in case we're shooting."

"God knows."

"Bob, whatever the film makes will go toward buying ambulances. We got the 12th Brigade's counterattack on the Arganda Bridge. Some great tank sequences."

"The tanks weren't any good there," said the officer. "Tomorrow we'll be much better." He emptied his glass, put it down. "I think I need a bath now," he said.

Delmer emerged from the barbershop, walked through the hall. He stopped for a moment to speak with the whores waiting in the halls for customers. They burst into loud laughter. Delmer made a face and went over to Ernest.

"*Leche* means milk, doesn't it?" he asked. The girls were giggling again.

"Among other things," said Hemingway.

"Sounds lewd. What else does it mean?"

"It sounds lewd, it looks lewd." Ernest beckoned to Caminea, one of the girls. She was dressed almost demurely, but with a phony French elegance. She laughed and ran her fingers through Delmer's thin hair.

"Stop laughing at me," said the fat man.

She pretended to pout. "I'm not making fun of you, my little roly-poly. It's the *leche* that's funny."

"How's business?" Ernest asked.

Caminea pointed over to a few soldiers who were shooting dice in a corner. "Look at them," she said. "The boys would rather gamble away their money than spend it on something better."

"Like what?"

"*Leche!*"

Ernest reached into his pocket, gave her a few peseta notes, whispered, "Be nice to them, Caminea. They've been fighting all day, and tomorrow they have to go back."

She put the money in her little bag. "Don Ernesto," she said, "you take care of your Lincoln Brigades just like a father."

Carminea went to the other girls and led them over to the soldiers. A few minutes later they all disappeared upstairs. Ernest and Delmer headed toward the restaurant. On the way they walked past an American journalist phoning in a story. Ernest couldn't help listening.

"Madrid is in the grip of terror. It can be felt everywhere. Innocent citizens are being arrested in the streets by the secret police, they're being tortured and killed. Bodies are everywhere."

Ernest shot Delmer a look. "Do you know him?"

"Came last night. Hasn't left the hotel since."

Ernest shook his head. Taking Delmer by the arm, he pushed him through the restaurant.

There were not many people in the restaurant and the atmosphere was gloomy. Ernest sat at a table with Delmer and his film crew, poking at his meal.

"Water soup with millet," he groaned. "Yellow rice with horse meat. What grub! The waiters here are nothing but corrupt war profiteers."

"They're tipped much too high," said Delmer.

"They slaughtered a cow in the American Embassy," Ernest announced. "The porter called me a while ago and said they'd put aside ten pounds for us. I'll have it picked up tomorrow. We can cook up in my room."

Delmer nudged Ernest and nodded toward the door. The American journalist, his report finished, was entering the room. Delmer waved him over to their table, and he sat down facing Ernest, who asked politely, "How do you like Madrid?"

"I like it."

"How long have you been here?"

"Since last night."

Ernest retained his polite tone. "And where did you see the corpses that are supposed to be lying around everywhere?" Ernest turned to two journalists, Gustav Regler and Dr. Werner Heilbrun, at the next table. "I heard him calling in his story," he said, his voice changing. "He says Madrid's in a grip of terror, that the police are dragging innocent people from the streets, torturing and killing them."

The journalist paled.

"You don't know a goddamned thing!" Ernest bellowed. "But we know you're a liar, that you're spreading lies. And I'm going to find out why and for whom." He stood. "Even if I have to knock it out of you."

The journalist backed off. As Ernest made a move to follow him, Delmer grabbed his sleeve. "Hem, calm down."

"I'd like nothing better than to sock him one." Ernest sat down. John Dos Passos came up to the table and took a seat. He was anxious, alarmed.

"Robles has been arrested! I kept telling him to get out of Spain, but he wouldn't listen to me."

"Take it easy, Dos," Ernest said. "Who's Robles?"

"My translator. Professor in English. His son called me. He was picked up off the street."

Ernest turned back to his meal. "Shouldn't have taken up with the Fascists," he said. "You'll find another interpreter."

Dos Passos grabbed Hemingway by the arm, almost spilling his rice. "Ernest! Robles is a colonel in the Republican army! He's not a Fascist, dammit!"

"Well? What was he up to?" Ernest went on eating.

"His brother is with the Fascists. That's what he's up to."

Ernest shrugged. "If that's all it is, nothing will happen to him."

"I've heard he's already been shot!" said Dos Passos.

"People talk too much."

Dos Passos looked around at the others. "You've got to help me!" he implored. He looked at Mikhail Koltsov, a Russian reporter for *Pravda*. "Comrade Koltsov, what's happened to Robles?"

Koltsov, mid-fifties, balding and shortsighted, removed his glasses and cleaned them meticulously with his handkerchief. He smiled politely. "Whatever do you mean, Comrade Dos Passos? I am only a simple jouralist."

Dos Passos stared him down. "Everyone knows you do more than just report for *Pravda*. You must help me!"

The others looked at Koltsov expectantly. Koltsov looked past them to the entrance. In the doorway, tall, slim, blond, was Martha Gellhorn. She wore gray flannel trousers, a sweater, and a warm windbreaker. On her back was a knapsack. Ernest saw her and went over to where she was standing.

"I knew you'd get here, daughter," he said. "And do you know why? Because I arranged it."

He led her to the table.

"This is Martha Gellhorn," he said to the journalists. "She's a passionate war correspondent and an anti-Fascist. She writes for *Colliers*, a magazine with over a million readers."

Beaming proudly, he introduced her to his colleagues, ending with Gustav Regler. "Regler here has just recently fled from Germany. I'm glad he's here. Sometimes it's easy to forget that not all Germans are Nazis."

Martha shook hands with Regler and the others. She spoke a few words to them in fluent German. They were surprised.

"I lived for a while in Nazi Germany," she explained. "I wanted to write a book about the rise of National Socialism."

"That's why Heilbrun and I and some other Germans are fighting here. So the world will stop hating all Germans for what the Nazis are doing," said Regler.

Hemingway excused himself and Martha, took her to the reception desk and watched her check in. His mood had lifted, he was laughing again.

* * *

The hotel manager accompanied them up the broad staircase to the third floor. He opened the doors to a few rooms in the rear, most of them more like storage closets and servants' rooms. Martha shook her head indignantly.

The manager shrugged. "That's the best I can do. Five dollars a night."

Martha shook her head.

"Ah, too expensive for you?" He walked to the other side of the corridor, opened a door to an elegant, large drawing room. "This is the cheapest I can offer you. One dollar a night."

Amazed, Martha regarded him. "I'll take it," she said.

"As you like."

He and Ernest exchanged looks. Ernest nodded, winked.

*   *   *

She unpacked her knapsack, placing her clothing in neat piles on the bed. As Ernest observed her, she added more and more cakes of soap to an already conspicuously large pile. She was nervous from her trip and spoke quickly.

"Then I got the train to Barcelona. Full of young soldiers. They gave me garlic sausage and wine and they taught me songs. We sang and drank the whole way. And when we got here, can you believe it? The taxi driver refused to take any money from me. I was passed around like a parcel, from one person to the next. It was wonderful."

Ernest regarded the pile of soap. "What's all this?"

"Soap. I heard it was scarce."

"Food is scarce. Everyone who passes through Paris brings back a knapsack full of food." They laughed.

Suddenly there were sounds of rifle and machine-gun fire, then a grenade launcher. The explosions came closer. Martha was startled. Ernest went to her, pointed out the window.

"See over there? Garabitas Hill. That's where the Fascist positions are. They spray the whole city from up there."

"You mean they can reach us here?"

"We've been hit thirty times in the past few weeks."

"What's that funny smell?"

"Explosives. A mortar round just went off in the courtyard."

"My God," she said. "What'll we do?"

"Get used to it. You wanted a room in the front."

* * *

That night Martha lay alone in her bed, trying to sleep. The battle sounds outside kept getting louder. She got up, went to the balcony door, and closed it. She ran back to bed and curled up in a corner. Grenades flew over the hotel and exploded nearby. Plaster fell from the ceiling. The small lamp on the bedside table began to tremble. Martha sat up, threw her bathrobe over her shoulders, and hurried to the door. It was locked. She rattled the handle.

"Open up! Open up, help!"

She listened. Nothing. She began pounding the door with her fists. "Open up, help!"

A stray bullet crashed through the window and hit a large mirror. Martha screamed. In total panic she pounded on the door. Suddenly it opened from the outside. Standing there in his pajamas, a bathrobe slung over his shoulders, was Ernest. The emergency lights, dim and flickering, were turned on in the corridor, giving everything a weird glow. Martha regained some of her composure.

"Oh, Ernest, I tried to get out and the door was

locked. From the outside. Someone must have locked me in by accident."

Ernest grinned. "I think it's safe to assume that whoever locked you in meant well."

"But why?"

"So you couldn't run out on me."

A little later they were lying together in bed, both of them wide awake. The battle sounds had died down. Martha snuggled up close to Ernest. He caressed her tenderly.

"You don't have to be afraid," he said. "The front's seventeen blocks away."

"I'm not afraid," she assured him.

"Hear that? *Ta-crong, ca-pong, cong ta-crong*—those are heavy machine guns, fifty caliber. If you can hear the shots, most of the time they're already past."

"Great."

"Hear that? *Cong, ca-rong, rong, rong*—that's a light machine gun."

"I have a queer feeling in my stomach."

"You're hungry. Have some soap."

"No, I'm afraid. What was that?"

"Grenade launcher. *Shwui, shwui!* Sounds like a lion coughing." He looked at Martha. "Ever hear a lion cough?"

She shook her head. Suddenly there was a shattering explosion, very close. Glass broke, plaster fell from the ceiling. Petrified, Martha sat bolt upright.

"What was that?"

"A direct hit."

They held each other closely until the battle sounds faded entirely, and they went to sleep.

* * *

Morning. A wounded woman was carried into the hotel lobby and laid on the floor. She was bleeding badly. Curious hotel guests in pajamas and robes stood around on the landings. Ernest and Martha came down the steps with Dr. Heilbrun, who carried his doctor's bag. Kneeling next to the wounded woman, he took her pulse. There was none. He closed her eyes. Martha looked at the dead woman, horrified.

Dr. Heilbrun took Ernest aside. "We must return to our units," he said.

He hugged Ernest, who returned the hug, then kissed the doctor—almost tenderly—on both cheeks.

"Take care of yourself, comrade," said Hemingway. When Regler approached, he hugged him just as hard. "Keep your eye on the doctor here. We'll all get together soon, eh?"

"One can never count on that," Regler said.

"Hey, none of that now!" In spite of everything, Hemingway was in a good mood. He gave Martha a hug, nodding toward the Germans who were on their way out. "Now, there are two men who don't give up."

"Like you," she said.

* * *

They were having coffee and eggs with Dos Passos and the film crew in the big hotel restaurant when the film director, spoke his mind.

"We have to show how Madrid is being defended by all its inhabitants," he said. "The workers, the farmers, the intellectuals, everyone fighting together to defend democracy and Spain's independence."

"Right," said the camera operator. "But we can't ignore the youth organizations. We have to show positive things, like the way the Moroccans have joined the people's struggle. And then there are the working-class sections and the proletarian armies in the factories."

Dos Passos had to laugh. "I'm sure the American public will be extremely interested in all those things," he said sarcastically. "No, what we really have to show is the way this war is making the people suffer, the privations of everyday life. We could concentrate on a village in old Castile! That would be far better than chasing around after day-to-day propaganda at the front."

"Dos, the only way to shake up the people in America," Hemingway objected, "is to give them horrible images. Attacks, bombardments, destruction—not life in some peaceful village. The people are fighting for Madrid, not Alicante or Almería."

"The people stopped fighting a long time ago," said Dos Passos.

"Yes?" Ernest was irked. "And who's been holding off the Fascists?"

Dos Passos leaned forward. "Since Stalin got into the act a lot of innocent people are being pulled off the street and shot."

Ernest winked at Martha. "He's getting worked up. But the truth of the matter is he's just concerned about his Spanish translator, Robles, and not about the cause."

"I don't see any difference," Dos Passos snapped. "Where's Robles? You tell me."

Ernest lowered his voice. "There are people who ask a lot of questions. It's not good to ask too many questions."

Now Dos Passos was furious. "I'll ask as many questions as I damn well like! And I won't stop asking until I've found him!"

"Quintanilla," said Ernest. "Head of antiespionage. He gave me his word that Robles will get a fair trial."

Dos Passos was incredulous. "Quintanilla? He's a butcher, Ernie! The man has people murdered!"

"And what if there is something to the charges?"

Dos Passos clenched his fist. "Charges? Nobody even knows what the charges are! And I thought you were my friend." He left the table without another word.

Later that day Ernest and Martha were joined by the Russian reporter, Koltsov, on the rooftop terrace of the hotel. The shelling had stopped and many buildings were on fire.

"I am sorry for Dos Passos," said Koltsov. "But Robles has been shot."

Ernest was startled by the news. "Shot? Without a trial?"

"I'm afraid so."

"Dos Passos was right," said Ernest. "That isn't war. It's political murder."

Koltsoz spoke calmly. "You have to get used to the idea that war kills innocent people, comrade."

"No. The international brigades came to Madrid to fight for a just cause, not to hunt down spies and shoot innocent people," Ernest said.

Koltsov shrugged. "The international brigades? Thirty-five thousand men. Insignificant. We are trying to form a Spanish army of twenty times that number. The brigades are nothing more than propaganda."

Martha spoke up. "Is that what you write for *Pravda*?" she asked.

Surprised, Koltsov looked at Martha. "It's not my job to write about what happens here in Spain, Miss Gellhorn. I write about what *should* happen. For *Pravda*, the international brigades are comprised of brave members of the international working class."

"That's pure propaganda," said Martha.

"We are not objective reporters," replied the Russian. "We have reached out to all parties, regardless of whether they write or make films."

Martha fastened him with a look. "On my way back from the telephone office I saw people standing in line for food. As I was watching, a grenade landed right next to them and exploded. The people didn't move. Nobody dared leave their place in line."

"And the moral to your little story?"

"That the hunger in the city is stronger than the fear," she said.

"There is no hunger in Madrid," said Koltsov. "That is what we must report."

"Lies? Why?" she demanded.

"Out of solidarity for the cause."

Heatedly, Ernest objected. "But it's not the same thing to show solidarity for people's suffering and Russian interests?"

Koltsov held up a finger. "It is in all our interests," he said, "to spur the Spanish cause on to victory. This struggle will determine whether Fascism is to engulf Europe and the entire world."

Ernest shook his head. "I'm not a Communist, comrade, and I'll never be one," he said evenly. "I believe in freedom, not ideologies. Do you really think that the Spanish workers in the cities and the peasants in the fields are fighting here for the future of Europe? No. They're fighting for their country, because it belongs to them. They're fighting for the Spanish earth!"

New York—Summer, 1937

On the big screen in Carnegie Hall, the final sequence played to a hushed house. Along with the startling images was Ernest Hemingway's voice:

Over footage of the street in simple, clear words he described the victory won by the untrained civilians. The people who only wanted the basics of life— work and food—have bravely learned to fight and are carrying on the courageous battle.

The screen became dark. Ernest and Martha were standing in the wings, listening to the sustained applause of 3,000 spectators. Ernest pulled at his tie, loosened his collar.

"They're waiting for you," said Martha. She gave

him a kiss and a little shove. He stepped out onto the stage and was received by deafening applause. Blinded by the spotlights, he took off his glasses and squinted at the audience. He walked slowly to the dais, over which was hung a huge banner with the words LEAGUE OF AMERICAN WRITERS * SECOND CONGRESS, 1937. Silence descended, then Ernest began to speak.

"Fascism is a lie fabricated by tyrants. A writer who doesn't want to lie can neither live nor write under Fascism. Because Fascism is a lie, it is condemned to literary sterility. And when it has disappeared one day, the only story it will have inherited is the bloody story of murder."

In the wings Martha watched with admiration as Ernest warmed to his subject.

"I began by talking about how difficult it is to write well and honestly, and about the inevitable reward for those who succeed in doing so. It is very dangerous to write the truth in a war, and it is also very dangerous to get at the truth. Thank you."

Martha threw her arms around his neck when he went to her. "You were wonderful!" she exclaimed. "We can't lose with you on our side!"

Freeing himself from her embrace, Ernest tried to make out the person standing by her side. It was Dos Passos. Amazed, Ernest stared at him.

"What are you doing here?"

"I'm a writer," said Dos Passos. "Just like you."

Ernest was angered. "How much did they pay you to betray Spain and the cause?" he demanded.

Dos Passos shrugged off the insult. "Ernie, it stopped being a war against Fascism when the Russians took over. It turned into a purge against the anarchists, the Trotskyites, the socialists—everyone and everything the Russian generals are afraid might not fit in with the Kremlin's plans."

"Lucasz is Hungarian!" Ernest snapped. "Petrov's Bulgarian, Merriman's American, Walter's a Pole, and Heilbrun's German. Sorry, Dos, no Russians there."

"Heilbrun's dead," Dos Passos announced.

The sentence was like a slap in the face. At a complete loss, Ernest looked at his old friend. Dos Passos looked down. "He was flying back to the front. His plane was hit by machine-gun fire. I'm sorry, Ernie."

Ernest looked at Martha. There were tears in her eyes. He walked away, went back to the empty hall, sat down on a bench. He cried softly. Martha came up and sat beside him. She took his hand, but he pulled it back.

"I'm sorry," she said. "I know how much you loved that man. I thought I knew everything about this war. Not true. I didn't know it kills your friends."

He took her hand and held it tightly. "Do you remember how bad it was and how tired we were, so tired that it hurt? And the way we were always hungry?"

"Yes. And you and your whiskey. And the raw onions, even in the morning."

"And the heat and the dust," said Ernest. "And always being thirsty." He looked at her. "Martha, I'm going to write about it. The truth, the way it really was. For all those who died for something they believed in. I'm going back. Will you come with me?"

"I wouldn't let you go alone," she said.

"I want to tell you something. I love you."

"And I love you." She put her arm around him. "I love your broad shoulders and your funny way of walking, like a gorilla. With you it's like being in a snowstorm, only the snow is warm and it never melts."

"Will you marry me? Or at least stay at my side, always, wherever I go?"

Martha shook her head. "I'd like to, Ernest. But what about Pauline?"

"What about her?"

"She's your wife."

He looked away, shrugged. "Pauline and I grew apart a long time ago."

And that, thought Martha, is that.

Key West—Fall, 1937

Ernest stood before a wooden bookcase, carefully leafing through the books, sorting them, stacking them together. He put the lid on his portable typewriter, took his pencils, pens, notebooks, and erasers from the desk drawer. Pauline, a large drink in hand, stood in the doorway watching. She looked different. Her hair was bleached blond, down to her shoulders. She had put on a little weight. Her presence did not seem to distract Ernest.

"Where can I reach you?" she asked.

"Your best bet's care of Ambos Mundos in Havana," he said over his shoulder.

"I mean by telephone," she said. "In case something comes up, someone asks for you."

"We don't have a telephone."

"How cozy."

He said nothing, went on sorting his blue notebooks.

"But there must be somewhere I can forward your mail." Pauline was drinking much too quickly, jiggling the glass so the ice cubes clinked.

"Send it to the same address."

"And? Has she already staked out a little love nest?"

"Up in the mountains," he replied casually. "Seventeen miles outside Havana. *Finca Vigía*. There's a spectacular view of the bay and the whole sea. A wonderful place to work, where the boys can spend their summer vacations."

Pauline raised her voice. "The boys. You couldn't care less about the boys. You use them the way you used me, like you use everyone around you."

He faced her. "And you're using them right now . . . to hurt me," he said.

Pauline looked away.

"The boys enjoy being with me," said Ernest. "I want them to come." He placed some books in a large leather traveling bag. Pauline paced back and forth restlessly.

"They're coming with me to my sister's this summer," she said flatly.

Ernest put his hands on his hips. "Pauline, we've already decided that the boys would come to visit me this summer. And we agreed not to fight over them."

She emptied her glass. She was about to leave when she stopped, turned around, and began speaking softly, as though she were speaking to herself.

"You hate me, don't you? Because I took you away from Hadley, and because I'm rich—and you feel like you sold out to me."

He turned around and looked at her in amazement. "What ever put that into your head?" he asked.

"That's the way you write about me, isn't it? And all the while you know it isn't true. That's never the way it was between us. We loved each other. What did I do to make you hate me so?"

"I don't hate you, Pauline."

She looked at him hopefully, almost pleadingly. "Then, you've written me off."

Ernest turned back to his packing. He shrugged. "What you can't stand is that I'll be living with someone else while I write an incredibly good book."

There was a pause, then, "Do you remember what Scott once told you?"

"No."

"He said you need a new wife for each new book."

Ernest nodded, went on packing.

Cuba—Spring, 1938

The one-story Colonial-style house was located on the perimeter of a large, overgrown tropical park. Martha sat on the veranda, reading a manuscript. Ernest emerged from a small doorway that led to his study. He smiled, looking at her, rubbed his hands together.

"Marty," he said, "you're fiendishly beautiful. And me, I'm the happiest man on earth."

Martha lowered the manuscript and held out her hand. Ernest walked over, took her hand, and kissed it. He sat down next to her in a rocking chair.

She closed the manuscript. "I wouldn't let any of the comrades see the massacre chapter," she said. "It's good, but gruesome."

"Ha! Let the comrades worry about party discipline. I'm not bound to do anything. All I want to do is write, to put it down just the way I saw it."

"They'll rip you apart."

"Just let 'em try." He sat up, shouted into the house, "Juan! Two thirsty people here. Bring out the shaker with the martinis!"

"You're making good progress?" she asked.

"Four hundred and sixty words."

Juan, the houseboy, arrived with a tray and drinks. Ernest looked at him and laughed. "Why are you always in such a hurry?" he demanded. "You think we're a couple of drunks who can't wait?" Juan laughed as he served the drinks.

"Is everything all set for the boys?" he asked the servant.

"Oh yes, sir. Everything, and two extra cases of soda."

Martha sipped her drink. "How old is Bumby now?"

"Fifteen," he replied. "You'll really like him. A great kid."

"And the little one?"

"Not so little anymore. Pat's eleven. He's very trusting. Has a sense of justice. Sometimes he can be a real nuisance when he badgers the others. The boys stick up for each other. Sometimes they fight, and then they make up. They're really very proud of each other."

"And do you think they'll accept me? Another woman for Papa's big family?"

* * *

Ernest sat at his huge desk, writing. Bright sunlight poured in through the wide-open window. It was hot and he wore only shorts and an open shirt. He wrote with a pencil on a thick notebook of unlined paper. He crossed out a line, reflected, stared at the paper, then continued writing. Outside on the veranda, where the coffee table was already set, he could hear his children's voices.

"What do you guys think?" Pat asked. "I think she's beautiful," said he. "She *is* beautiful."

"I think she likes us," Bumby added.

Pat giggled. "You've fallen in love with her!"

"How about you?" Bumby asked.

"I don't fall in love so easy," Pat replied.

Ernest listened, went on writing. Then he heard Martha's voice.

"Morning, boys."

"Good morning, Miss Gellhorn," they said in unison.

Ernest laughed. Then he lost himself in his work.

* * *

Ten minutes later Patrick was standing next to his father's desk, watching. Ernest was counting the words he had written.

"I thought you were writing, Pa," he said.

"I am."

"But you're doing arithmetic problems."

"I'm counting how many words I've written."

"Why?"

"So I'll know how much I've written."

"But you can see that right there on the paper."

Ernest sat back and smiled at his son. "But you see, once I've counted, I can then go around and tell everybody the number. At the end of the week I add everything together and then I tell myself I'm a super writer and not some jerk. It's great being a writer, Patrick. You should try it some time."

"Aw, I don't know . . ."

Ernest stood up. "Come on," he said, "let's go fishing!"

* * *

Ernest stood on the flying bridge of the *Pilar,* steering the boat through dark blue water. Bumby stood next to him, a grown boy, thrilled to be with his famous father.

"The water's so blue," said Bumby. "Just like you see in the ads."

"Power of suggestion," said Ernest. "They tint the color in the ads. You get down here and the color looks different. It's really the same damn blue anywhere."

"Really?"

Ernest laughed, clapped Bumby on the back. "Just kidding. Seeing if you're on your toes."

"You didn't fool me."

"I know. The water's this color because of the salt in it. The shades vary with the depth. The deeper it is the darker blue."

Ernest looked aft, where the trolled bait was skipping in the boat's wake. Patrick sat in one of the two fighting chairs, holding a rod, waiting for a strike.

"La vie est belle avec Papa," Bumby said.

Ernest looked at him and chuckled. "Do you still remember Paris? The apartment over the sawmill, and

Mr. Featherpuss? I took you to the Closerie des Lilas in the stroller. I read the newspaper and you kept guard."

"What did we eat for breakfast?"

"Brioche et cafe au lait."

"And for me?"

"I believe you had a beer."

Bewildered, Bumby looked at his father, who laughed.

"You were a big beer drinker, kiddo," Ernest said. "For dinner you preferred red wine with water. But every once in a while you enjoyed a little absinthe, too."

Suddenly Carlos Gutiérrez, cook and mate, let out a shout.

"Fish! Here he comes! Patrick, watch out!"

The fish took Patrick's bait. His line tautened and whipped the water. "I got him!" yelled the boy. The rod bent, the line ran out. Ernest cut the motor.

"It's a sailfish!" he shouted. "I saw his sail when he cut the water!"

Carlos took the back off Pat's chair and strapped the harness across his waist. Bracing his feet against the footrest, he yanked the rod against the fish's weight, using all his strength. "Oh God, I think I've got him!" he exclaimed.

Ernest started the engine, spun the boat in a neat semicircle. "Everything okay, Mouse?"

Patrick was panting, out of breath, winding the reel for all he was worth. "Oh, God, please let me get him . . ."

Suddenly the line tautened, then ran out with a shrieking sound. Carlos put the broad cushion of the hip harness around Pat's narrow shoulders, fastened the harness strap crosswise over it. "Now you can hold him with your back and shoulders," said the mate. "You okay?"

"Thirsty! Can I have some water?"

Carlos ran below and returned with a glass. Everyone was excited.

"Just tell me what to do," Patrick said. "I'll do it, even if it kills me."

Pat reeled in the line. Bracing himself, he pulled with his arms, shoulders, back, and thighs.

Bumby looked from the small boy to their father. "Think he can handle that fish?" he asked.

"He's doing beautifully! Look, I think it's running in."

"He's coming!" shouted Carlos. "The beast is coming!"

The big fish burst from the water, jumped, silver and dark blue, a flash. For a second it seemed to hover in midair, then it fell back to the surface with a huge splash.

"My God!" yelled Pat. "A monster!"

"At least a ton!" shouted Carlos.

"He threw up so much water!" said Bumby.

Ernest was awestruck. "Have you ever in your life seen anything so blue and wonderfully silver? Now reel in your line, Mouse!"

Pat strained, raising and lowering the rod, winding furiously when the fish ran in, letting the drag do the work when the monster ran away.

Bumby was concerned. "Papa, Pat's feet are bleeding, his hands . . ."

"And if it were your fish?" asked his father.

"I'd fight him till I dropped."

Ernest spoke so they all could hear: "If Patrick gets him he'll have something for the rest of his life, something here inside that'll make everything else a little easier. Sometimes boys have to go through this sort of thing if they're going to become men."

"He's great. I'm sure it'll do him good," said Bumby. Then he added, "I know he's your favorite. Otherwise you'd stop him."

"Carlos wouldn't let him go if it were too much for him, Bumby." Then Ernest lowered his voice. "Why do you think he's my favorite?"

"Isn't he?"

"I've loved you longest."

Harpoon in hand, Carlos bent over the stern. "Watch it, Patrick!" he shouted. "The hook's hanging on by a hair! Hold him! My God, the hook's out!"

Patrick fell backward. The line came out of the water—empty.

The boy collapsed. A few minutes later he lay naked, on his stomach, on a blanket. Carlos rubbed his limbs, massaged him with alcohol. Ernest brought him a fresh shirt and dry jeans.

"I'm okay, Papa," Pat said, rolling over.

Ernest nodded. "I know how you feel."

"Nobody knows that."

"I'm sorry he got away," said his father. "I've never seen anyone fight a fish so magnificently."

"Papa, when it got so hard that I could hardly go on, I didn't know anymore who was who, him or me. Then I loved him, more than anything in the world."

"I see."

"I don't mind that he got away, Papa. I'm glad he's okay. I'm okay, too. We're not enemies."

Ernest smiled proudly. "It's good to hear you say that, Son."

At dusk, with the boys asleep in their beds in the guest house, Ernest went to the veranda, where Martha was waiting for him. On the table was a tray with drinks. Ernest picked up some of the boys' clothing that was lying about, and eyed the glasses.

"You really enjoy the boys," said Martha.

"Yes, I do. And you know, they're very taken with you."

"I'm glad. How's Patrick?"

"I think he's okay. He's sleeping. I didn't think it would take so much out of him."

"Guilty conscience?"

Ernest nodded. Martha handed him a martini. "A bad conscience should have something to swim in," she said.

Ernest drank slowly, deliberately, as though he were taking medicine. "I'm just sorry they'll have to be leaving soon. The time's gone by so quickly."

Martha's expression changed. Apprehensively she took up a letter and handed it to him. "It from *Colliers*. They want me to cover the war in Finland. I'm not sure if I should go."

Stunned, Ernest read the letter. He was pale when he turned back to her. "Is it because of money? Because if it is, you know you don't have to . . . I don't want you to go, Martha."

"I've never asked you for money," she reasoned. "I've always managed on my own. That gives me the right to go off and earn my own living." There was just a trace of defiance in her voice.

"Okay," said Ernest. "You want to be independent, that's fine. You have your savings. You can write and sell short stories. You don't have to knock around as a reporter anymore."

"I don't think of it as 'knocking around.'"

Ernest didn't answer.

"I hate the thought of leaving you," she said lamely.

"Then, why do it?" Ernest poured her and himself another martini, downing his in one gulp.

"It's what I have to do."

"Oh," he said.

Martha went to him and took his hand. "You know I love you."

Ernest nodded. "If anyone asks, I'll say I'm bankrupt and you had to go off to war to make money so I can finish my novel."

She stroked his cheek. "Have you decided on a title?"

Again he nodded, solemnly. "Any man's death diminishes me, because I am involved in mankind. And therefore never send to know for whom the bell tolls. It tolls for thee."

"For thee and me," said Martha.

* * *

Ernest was at his usual position on the short side of an L-shaped counter in the Floridita Bar in Havana. It was still morning and the room was only partially filled. Guests came in for a quick drink, a look around. A few whores were waiting for their clients, and one of the girls, Betty, a somewhat corpulent, older, but still pretty woman, sat by Ernest's side. Hemingway was drinking reflectively, staring into the bartender's glass as if it were a crystal ball.

"Joseph," he said to the bartender, "another double daiquiri without sugar."

"Trying to break your record?" asked the bartender as he made the drink.

"No," said Ernest. "I just want a quiet drink."

"Ha," said Joseph, filling his glass. "You said that when you set your record. It's 11:30. You're making excellent time. I think you have a good chance."

"Hey, lay off with the record already," said Betty.

"You're in good shape today," he said to Hemingway. "You're drinking good and steady, and it's not having any effect."

"To hell with the record," Ernest said.

"I'm keeping count anyway."

"Ernie can count, Joseph," said Betty. Then she looked at Ernest. "Say something. Tell me something."

Ernest sipped his drink, held the liquid in his mouth a long time before swallowing. Then, "Well now, Betty, what shall I tell you? What do you want to hear?"

"Whatever you want, whatever occurs to you. Are you happy."

"Ask a man if he's happy and he ceases to be," said Hemingway, quoting Voltaire.

"Were you happy before I asked you if you were happy?"

"No."

"Tell me about when you *were* happy?"

"In the Alps," said Ernest, growing animated. "When I'd get up in the morning and it was quiet . . . and the maid lit the fire in the tiled stove . . . and there was snow outside. And the dog—Schnauz—was there, and Mr. Bumby on his sled. And there was a woman that I loved. We had a beautiful time, and I was happy. Happier than ever."

"Happier than with other women?"

"I was very happy, desperately happy. So happy that I couldn't stand it. I ran away from it all . . . out of happiness."

"Like the way you're happy now with your long-legged blond?"

"The blond? No. She's bent on running around in the fog. Sailed across the North Sea. In Europe writing about the war for *Colliers*. Make money. And if the ship runs into a mine and goes down, the magazine will pay at least double. Maybe they'll even let me write her obituary."

He looked up. Martha was standing in the doorway. How long had she been there? His face assumed an innocent expression.

"Hi, Marty," he said. "Want a drink?"

On their way home to the finca Ernest sat beside Martha, who was behind the wheel of the Lincoln convertible. She was not in the best of moods.

"You know, Scrooby," she said, "you should really bathe a little more and drink a little less."

"Yeah? Maybe you should bathe a little less and drink a little more."

She paused; then, "Listen. I'm not abnormally

clean. But in that respect you're one of the least ambitious men I've ever known."

Ernest said nothing.

"You haven't finished a book in three years. You're not writing now. If you're not writing, what are you?"

"I'll write again."

"Well, I've been thinking about the *Colliers* offer."

"I know."

"Ernie, why don't we go back together? Like we did in Spain. The war's waiting for us in Europe, where we can really contribute something. Nothing could be more important than crushing Hitler."

"The war's going on here, too."

Martha laughed. "When I'm away from you I long to go back. But when I'm here . . . Ernie, the people you associate with, the constant drinking, the filth, the way you live . . . it makes me sick."

No reply. Ernest stared out into the dark night.

"So," she said decisively, "I'm going to take the job."

"Stay with me." He didn't want it to sound like a plea, but it was.

"I'm going," she said. "I can't go on living like this."

His mood turned; anger toned his voice. "Are you crazy? Are you just looking for trouble? Don't you have any sense of responsibility?"

She drove, saying nothing.

"I forbid you to go back. Do you hear me? Do you hear?" He began to shout.

With the back of his hand he slapped her face. Martha let out a little cry. She yanked the wheel to one side and the car left the road, spinning into a meadow. She got out of the car and ran back to the road.

Ernest laughed out loud. He called to her. "If you go, if you leave me . . . I'll whip your ass, daughter!"

* * *

Within a week Martha was packed and ready to go. Ernest went to her as she got in the car. He had accepted things the way they were.

He wanted to tell her to come back safe and sound but knew it would ring false.

She looked at him, then looked away.

Ernest took a deep breath, his expression grim. He felt like an Indian who was losing his squaw with a hard winter knocking at the door.

Martha did not speak. She turned away and smiled brightly, then got in the car. She waved to the servants who had assembled on the veranda. She glanced once more at Ernest but set her face stonily and said nothing.

She closed the door. Juan, the chauffeur, started the car. The big Lincoln drove through the gates. Martha waved again, and was gone.

* * *

Dazed, Ernest returned to the veranda and sat down. The cat, Bosie, a small black and white animal, went to him and jumped in his lap. Ernest stroked her fur. The cat purred.

He continued to stroke Bosie, rubbing her under her chin. Bosie settled herself in his lap.

He fumbled for one of the glasses next to him on the floor. Finding one with a few drops left in it, he sipped, petting the cat.

"Pity you don't drink, Bosie. Otherwise, you're a pretty good cat."

Bosie purred. Ernest sipped.

I should find myself another wife, Ernest thought. Then we can both fall in love with her. If you can feed her you can have her. But I don't know a single woman who'd put up with living exclusively on mice . . . or not very long.

Ernest grew sad.

"What am I going to do, Bosie? What am I going to do?"

The cat looked up at him, but merely blinked her eyes sleepily and continued to purr.

* * *

Late that night Ernest phoned Pauline in Key West. He chatted aimlessly about the weather for a while, asked about the boys, and tried to gage her mood. Finally, he plunged in and asked her if he could come for a visit.

Pauline caught her breath. "This must mean that your wife has run off. You think you can come back to me just because Martha's gone?"

"Martha hasn't left me. Not a chance! She gone back to Europe to cover the war."

Pauline could tell from his tone of voice that he was hiding the real state of his marriage. "It's too late for us now, much, much too late."

Ernest exploded, pounding the wall by the telephone. "I should never have married a rich woman."

Pauline made no reply. Ernest knew he'd gone too far. He tried to soften the moment. "You're a damn nice girl, Pauline. I'm sorry I said that. I'm sorry about everything. But you know how I am."

She was crying softly. "Yes," she said, "I know how you are."

They hung up.

Three

France—Spring, 1944

The provisional headquarters of the Second American Infantry Division were located in a French château dating from the Renaissance. In what was once the great hall, a young press officer spoke to a gathering of war correspondents, using wall maps and a pointer to indicate the immediate area.

"Gentlemen," he said, pointing to the village of Épernon, "the Second Infantry Division is currently located here—about sixty kilometers from Paris."

This concluded the press officer's talk. The journalists, who had been listening closely, began to bombard him with questions.

"I've heard that the Fifth Infantry Division is supposed to advance toward Rambouillet and Paris," said one. "True?"

"What about the Seventh Tank Division?" asked another.

"Is it true that General Eisenhower and General Bradley are going to let the Second French Tank Division under General Leclerc enter Paris first for diplomatic reasons?"

Bill Walton, who had been close to the Second Division since the Normandy invasion, spoke up. "General Patton's army is holding north of Paris. Some say he's waiting for Roosevelt to get here. Is it true that the president is planning to go marching at the head of the troops personally?"

Another correspondent chimed in. "There are rumors that Montgomery's going to fall in with the American sector and then join the victory march to the Place Concorde. True or not true?"

141

The young press officer spread his arms.

"Gentlemen, please," he said with a tired smile. "One question at a time."

* * *

Bill Walton and a few of his colleagues came down the curving granite stairway leading from the château to the courtyard. Coming toward them was Ernest Hemingway, wearing worn fatigues and a white towel around his neck. He offered Walton a sip from a silver flask.

"Why weren't you at the press conference, Ernie?" Walton asked.

Ernest shrugged. "They're all just fakes, phonies, and ballroom bananas. You'll never get anything out of them. Big waste of time."

They stepped out of earshot of the other reporters.

"Seen Martha lately?" Walton asked.

"Not for months," said Ernest. "It's funny. I was going crazy in Cuba without her. I couldn't write. So I decided to come over here and find her, stay with her. I found her all right, but by the time I did I was more involved with the war. I'd begun to write again. I realized I didn't need her."

"What do you need?"

"The writing," he said without a pause." It always comes first."

One of the other reporters approached them. A young man, he looked at Hemingway with awe. "Do you have any information we don't?"

"About what?"

"The liberation of Paris."

"Nope."

"Any idea who's holding back and who's going in first?"

"No idea," said Ernest. "But I know one thing for sure. Whoever's first, I'll be with him."

At that moment a small, good-looking woman,

blond, mid-thirties, wearing a war correspondent's uniform, walked up to Bill Walton and smiled. She greeted him heartily, paying no attention to Ernest.

"Now, what are you doing here, Mary?" he asked, returning her smile. "I thought you'd be hammering away at your typewriter. Dispatches have to be sent out in a few hours you know."

"I'm stuck, Bill," she said with a frown. "I need some background material. Maybe you can tell me how many calories are in the troops' daily rations."

"Sorry," he said.

She shrugged, walked by him. Then she turned, and for a moment her eyes rested on Ernest, appraisingly. She turned back to Walton. "It's not easy, Bill," she said. "Even right here in the middle of all the experts." Then she walked away.

Bill noticed Ernest's eyes following her. "That was Mary Welsh," he said. "A colleague of mine at *Time*. She's a very good writer."

"Make sure you introduce me next time," said Ernest.

Walton drew himself to attention and gave Hemingway a mock salute. "Ay ay, mon colonel!" he said.

Ernest walked over to one of the army troop transports parked in the courtyard, where a few young Frenchmen, some of them with bare chests, were waiting in the loading area. He spoke briefly with them in French. Like lightning they jumped from the truck and came to attention.

"Oui, mon colonel," said one, saluting.

Ernest signaled for them to follow. He walked over to a low building. On his way he was rejoined by Walton, who had witnessed the scene by the truck.

"Ernie, are you planning to use this bunch to take Paris on your own?"

"I might."

"Where'd you pick them up, anyway?"

"In the woods around Rambouillet. They say the

Germans have abandoned the city. We need some tanks and ammunition right away."

Amazed, Walton shook his head.

* * *

Ten minutes later, Ernest stood before Colonel Bruce, an OSS officer. Bruce was dressed in civilian clothes, whereas Ernest wore a uniform and a steel helmet. Bruce fixed him with a stern glare.

"Look here, Hemingway," he said. "You're a war correspondent, not a member of the fighting forces. Civilians aren't supposed to get involved in their own operations sixty miles in front of the Allied troops—and with tanks, to boot!"

Ernest feigned innocence. "Sir, I don't want to be a nuisance," he said. "I just thought I could be of some use."

"If it happens again you'll land in front of a military tribunal," said the colonel. "I'll personally see to it that you're sent home. Is that clear?"

Ernest came to attention. "Yes sir, colonel!"

Bruce nodded to the door. "Now bring them in."

Ernest turned on his heel and left the room. In a moment he was back, leading the resistance fighters into the colonel's office. Bruce stood up, mustered them suspiciously.

"Where did you get your weapons?" he asked one.

Marcel, their leader, shrugged his shoulders. He explained to the colonel, in French, that he spoke no English. Bruce, who knew not a word of French, asked Ernest to translate.

"The weapons were dropped by parachute, sir."

The colonel nodded. "All right. Ask them where the German positions are."

Ernest huddled with Marcel. The other Frenchmen joined in and it wasn't long before they were all talking at once, pointing to different spots on the wall map. Colonel Bruce became impatient. "Quiet!" he barked.

"*Silence!*" said Hemingway to his men.

"Well," said Bruce, exasperated. "What did they say?"

"That the Germans left Rambouillet at three o'clock this morning, but that the streets are still mined."

"Ask them where."

Ernest led the colonel to the map table. "Here," he said, tracing the map with his finger, "on the road from Épernon to Rambouillet. The street curves slightly uphill and then drops off here."

Dumbfounded, the colonel regarded Ernest. "Now how in hell do you know that, Hemingway?"

Ernest did not change his expression. "From bike rides and hikes twenty years ago," he explained. "Bike rides are the best way to get to know the countryside. You start sweating when it goes uphill."

Colonel Bruce laughed. He studied the map.

Ernest waited a moment, then spoke: "Sir, it would be best if you gave us a few of your men from the tank reconnaissance division. Just in case."

Bruce looked up from the map. He paced back and forth, considered, then made his decision. "Okay," he said. "But listen, Hemingway. Don't get caught. It'll be bad enough for me—but it'll be worse for you."

Again Ernest came to attention, saluted. "Thank you, Colonel," he said. He started for the door, but Bruce called him back.

"Mr. Hemingway?"

"Sir?"

"Good luck, *mon colonel*!"

* * *

That afternoon the small column came up over a rise in the rainy, muddy road and down a soft curve. Ernest, leading the way in an open Jeep, signaled to the

truck bearing his resistance fighters and to another
vehicle with antitank specialists.

"*Arrêtez!*" he ordered. The column stopped.

The street curved to the right. Ernest nudged Marcel, pointed to a smoking German tank in the middle of
the street. The hatch was open and a dead German
soldier was slumped half outside. In front of the tank
an American Jeep was tipped over, next to it the bodies
of several dead GIs.

The Frenchmen jumped from the truck and
gathered around Ernest and Marcel. Ernest ordered
them all into a ditch running parallel to the road. Ernest scrutinized the scene through binoculars. "A German tank," he said. "Looks like our boys got it before
they got theirs." He handed Marcel the binoculars.

"Seems quiet enough, *mon colonel*. Shall we take
a closer look?"

Ernest was about to move forward when the lieutenant of the antitank specialists held him back.
"Wait," he said softly. "It could be a trap. Sometimes
they're on remote control. The whole thing looks like a
setup to me. That tank could be stuffed with TNT. A
convoy comes down the street and the dynamite starts
flying. They wouldn't have a chance."

Ernest took his advice. Waving the men back to
their trucks, he crept forward with Marcel and the
lieutenant just behind. Crouching, they worked their
way down the ditch toward the tank. Everything was
quiet. The lieutenant was the first to climb up on the
German tank. He looked past the dead German soldier,
down into the tank. Ernest examined the dead body.
He froze.

"Lieutenant, come here."

He pointed to the soldier's dog tags, hanging from
his neck. They were American. "Something's wrong
here," he said.

At that moment, thinking the situation was safe,

the truck drivers began to advance slowly. Neither Ernest nor the lieutenant took notice.

They were looking at the dead man. There was a piece of thin wire running out of the soldier's sleeve. It led along the side of the tank, down to the ditch at the side of the road, and then up to the other side. An almost invisible wire was stretched across the road.

It was then that Ernest noticed the tank's cannon. It was pointed at the place where the trucks would hit the wire. He showed it to the lieutenant, who promptly jumped down the tank's hatch.

Ernest waved for the trucks to stop, but no one saw him. The front wheels of the big transport were almost at the wire. Suddenly the entire turret turned slightly to the left. When the truck's tires made contact with the wire, the cannon fired. The shell struck the road right next to the convoy. A fountain of earth rained down on the soldiers.

Ernest stood up, smiling. "Let's go!" he said.

* * *

The small square in front of Rambouillet's classic town hall was enclosed on two sides by a wrought-iron grille. At this point the paved streets met the park and bent sharply to the right, along the grille. The Hôtel Grand Veneur, a two-story building, was located on the street behind some tall shade trees. Ernest and his patrol, on foot, ran across the square to the hotel.

Ernest climbed up a sewage pipe and looked through a window. All the furniture was knocked over, pieces of paper strewn about. The Germans seemed to have been in quite a hurry to leave their command post in the hotel, and the city.

Brandishing a Colt .45 and followed closely by his men, Ernest ran in the hotel through the main entrance. The manager's terrified face appeared at the reception desk. Trembling, he held his hands over his head and looked around uncertainly, until he realized that the soldiers weren't Germans.

"*Mon Dieu,*" he said to Ernest. "And I thought the Germans had come back again!"

"When did they pull out?"

"This morning around three. I spent the whole night hiding in my wine cellar."

Ernest perked up. "Wine cellar?"

* * *

An hour later Ernest spread a large map on the wall of the room he had requisitioned on the second floor. Scattered around everywhere, on the floor, the double bed, and the chairs, were weapons—rifles, machine guns, mines, and bazookas. The manager opened a bottle of champagne and poured Ernest a glass.

"Ah," said Hemingway. "Moët Chandon. *Formidable.*"

The manager poured a little for himself.

"I want you to tell me everything you saw," said Ernest. "Everything's important."

The manager went to the map, pointed to the road leading to Paris. "They went in this direction, *mon colonel.* Toward Trappes and Versailles. About eight hundred men, four boom-booms, about twelve tanks."

"How many boom-booms?"

"Four exactly."

"Very good."

The manager raised his glass to Ernest. "To America and the Americans," he said. "*Vive la France!*"

* * *

That night Ernest was joined in his private command post by Colonel Bruce of the OSS. They were looking down into the hotel courtyard where the French resistance fighters were marching in step and singing:

*"Dix bis avenue Gobelin
Dix bis avenue Gobelin
Dix bis avenue Gobelin
That's where my Bumby lives . . ."*

Colonel Bruce looked at Ernest questioningly. "What's that they're singing?"

"A children's song I taught them. It was the baby-sitter's address when we used to live in Paris. If my little son Bumby got lost, all he had to do was sing the song and then someone would've dropped him off at avenue Gobelin."

Marcel entered the room, accompanied by an old man. Nodding to him, he spoke to Hemingway. "One of our men found him on the outskirts of the city. He says he knows where the German positions are."

They went to the wall map. The old man pointed.

"Here," he said in a sad and tired voice, "just on the other side of Trappes. These are the German anti-tank positions. And here, on the road to Paris, are four tanks."

"Did you actually see the tanks?" asked Ernest.

The old man came to attention.

"See them?" he said, holding up his arms. "I touched them with these hands."

* * *

As Hemingway and Colonel Bruce entered the hotel foyer a short time later they were met by a high-ranking French officer accompanied by two adjutants. The officer saluted. Bruce returned the salute.

"The Second Tank Division under General Leclerc will advance toward Rambouillet. The general requested me to establish contact with you. Would you please make available any information you have to my deputy, Colonel Richard."

The officer turned to the colonel standing next to him and spoke in French, assuming that neither Ernest nor Colonel Bruce could understand. He instructed Colonel Richard to get rid of all the Americans before General Leclerc arrived. He made various derogatory references to them, saying they were full of self-importance and "only wanted stories to write for their newspapers."

Ernest, who didn't miss a word, was furious. He kept his temper while Colonel Richard turned to them and spoke in English.

"Gentlemen," said Richard, "the commander has asked me to congratulate you on your excellent reconnaissance work."

Ernest blew up, in French.

"Tell your commandant," he said in flawless Parisian, "that if he has any questions concerning the enemy positions between here and Versailles he has only to ask the 'self-important Americans.'"

The French officer turned red.

Outside in the courtyard, after the French officers had gone, Ernest's Jeep, driven by his trusted Sergeant Pelkey, drove up from the opposite direction. Two young German soldiers were in the backseat, flanked by two Resistance fighters, Jean and Onesime.

"We caught these two," Jean reported to Hemingway. "They're probably from units broken up around Chartres. Some try to return to the German lines and continue fighting. They are the worst."

Ernest studied the prisoners' spiteful, unyielding faces.

"Can we shoot them, *mon colonel?*" Jean asked.

"No. We'll interrogate them and then send them back to the division. Bring them up to my room."

Jean was angry. "But that is crazy, *mon colonel*," he blurted. "They will have to be fed and housed. It makes me sick. I was there in the last week when the Germans tortured and then shot eleven of our men. I was among those who were kicked and beaten. And they would have killed me too if they'd known who I am."

"Did you capture them?"

Jean shook his head. "No. They just turned up."

"Then they're not your prisoners," said Hemingway.

Marcel joined the group. *"Mon colonel,"* he asked, "when does it start? When do we finally move out?"

Ernest explained their position carefully. "We have to wait until the army's gotten through," he said. "Then we can follow them in."

"Damn!" the Frenchman exclaimed. "My wife is waiting for me in Paris. Why must we wait here for the big brass to go in first?"

Ernest smiled. "Let's be polite and let them go ahead of us. We'll let them liberate Paris. But we'll beat them to the Ritz for the big celebration. Okay?"

"Oui, mon colonel."

* * *

The following day the hotel was besieged by American and English journalists who arrived in Rambouillet with the troops. Among the war correspondents lined up at the reception desk in hopes of getting a room were Bill Walton and Mary Welsh.

"Messieurs," said the manager at the top of his voice, "I regret that the hotel is completely occupied, sold out, *complet!*"

Ernest was sitting close by at a table, eating with his men. Spotting Bill Walton, he waved him over and asked him to join them.

"Love to," said Walton, "but first I need a room for the night, or at least a bed."

Ernest clapped him on the back. "You'll get a room; leave that to me. Pull up a chair!"

When Walton was seated, Ernest poured him a glass of red wine. They clinked glasses.

"The others are pretty mad at you," said Bill. "I mean, for taking over the whole hotel."

"Hey, listen," said Ernest. "I got here first, didn't I? And after all, my men are fighters. They need somewhere to sleep."

"Are you setting up headquarters or something?"

Ernest winked. "We just want to get the lowdown on the Krauts' whereabouts."

"You can't resist, can you, Ernie?"

"I can resist anything but temptation," Ernest said, quoting Oscar Wilde. "I want to be the first to Paris. I will be. Stick with me, Bill."

The other journalists were in a black mood. One of them walked over to Ernest's table. "The *patron* says that Mr. Big Shot here has requisitioned all the rooms." He leaned down toward Hemingway. "Seems Mr. Big Shot thinks he's something special because he's written a few books."

The correspondent then picked up an empty glass and the bottle which was on the table, and poured himself a glass.

"Maybe Mr. Big Shot thinks he owns the whole goddamn hotel!" he said. He laughed, but the rest of the room grew quiet.

Ernest wiped his mouth. Very calmly he rose, removed his jacket and draped it over the back of his chair. Reflectively he rolled up his shirt sleeves as he walked around the table to where the journalist was standing. Without warning he struck him sharply on the chin. The correspondent fell to the floor in a heap. Ernest looked at his right fist. Then he looked at all the other writers.

"I can't remember having invited him for a drink," he said.

He stared at the door. Standing there, the only woman in the room, was Mary Welsh. He cast Bill

Walton an imploring glance. Obligingly, Walton went over to Mary and brought her back to their table.

"This is Mr. Ernest Hemingway," he said by way of introduction. "He is the commander of this city and a reconnaissance expert who knows all the enemy positions in the area. He would like very much to meet you, Mary. I hope you don't mind if I leave the two of you alone."

Ernest offered her a chair. She shook her head.

"I'm afraid I have to get back to work. Nice to have met you, Mr. Hemingway."

Ernest stood, smiling. "Wait a minute," he said. "What do you do when you're not working?"

"My husband and the magazine see to it that I don't get too bored," she replied.

"You mean you're married?"

"You mean you're not?"

Ernest changed the subject rapidly. "Are you covering the advance?"

She shook her head. "No. Bill keeps the best tidbits for himself. I report from the rear."

"Too bad."

"Hopefully I'll make the grand finale and be there when we march into Paris," she said.

Ernest filled and raised his glass.

"To Paris! You have to promise that you'll celebrate the liberation of Paris with me. At the Ritz!"

"You're on," she said. Then she winked, and walked away.

Paris—Spring, 1944

Except for a burned-out German half-track in the middle of the street, Paris's magnificent Place Vendome was empty. Off in the distance individual shots could be heard, the detonation of a grenade, sporadic bursts of automatic fire, a siren. Then, from the direction of the Seine, came Ernest Hemingway in his Jeep and behind it a truck, carring his private army.

Ernest sprang from the Jeep as it pulled up before the closed double doors of the Ritz. He rang the bell. Before long a light went on, the door opened slightly, and the sleepy face of the hotel manager appeared.

"Ausiello?" Hemingway inquired, recognizing him.

The manager looked at him suspiciously. When he recognized Ernest his eyes lit up. He opened the door and threw his arms around him.

"Welcome, welcome, Monsieur Hemingway! Welcome to the Ritz!"

"Anybody here?"

"No one! The hotel is completely empty. The Germans did not leave until just a few days ago. But where is your baggage? I will have your rooms straightened up immediately, rooms for you and your friends!"

Ausiello helped the Resistance fighters unload the Jeep and the truck. Carrying them as if they were suitcases, the men brought rifles, sub-machine guns, machine guns, mines, and rocket launchers into the hotel, the elevator, and up into their private rooms.

When all their gear had been stowed, Ernest found his way to the bar. He sat on a stool and faced Ausiello, who took his place behind the counter.

"And what will it be, Monsieur Hemingway?"

"How many glasses will this bar hold?"

Without flinching the manager replied, "The last time it was fifty."

"Okay," said Ernest. "Let's get started."

A few hours later the bar was packed with correspondents. Ernest was still sitting on the same barstool, slightly drunk. Sitting next to him were Bill Walton and Ernest's old friend from Madrid, Tom Delmer.

"Well," said Hemingway, "we took—and held—

Rambouillet. We went out on patrols. We got information for that bungler Leclerc so he could push forward. Did reconnaissance on all the Kraut positions—roadblocks, mine fields, antiaircraft and antitank artillery, everything between Rambouillet and Paris."

Delmer slapped Ernest on the shoulder. "No doubt about it, Ernie," he said. "You liberated Paris!"

Ernest nodded modestly. "I held back even though I knew all the German positions, out of respect for the army. I let them go in first. It was a lot of fun, Tom. Shooting, fighting, nothing to eat, sleeping out in the rain on the floor of some barn, knocked on our asses like in the good old days in Madrid."

"You might be in trouble," Delmer warned him. "Some of the other correspondents didn't exactly appreciate what you did."

"The hell with them," said Ernest. "We saved some of our people."

"Just the same," said Delmer, "they'll report it. There'll be a big stink."

Just then Martha Hemingway appeared beside them. Ernest was surprised, but too drunk to show it. She looked rumpled in her American war correspondent's uniform, no makeup, her hair tied behind.

"Hello, Marty" was all he said.

Martha greeted Delmer as though they were old friends. Then Ernest recovered his power of speech.

"Martha, this is Bill Walton from *Time*. And Bill, this is Martha, my wife, who left me to cover the war. I followed her here. And I'm damn happy I did." He leaned close to his wife. "So where've you been knocking about the last couple of weeks?"

"After the Normandy invasion I took a hospital ship back to England. Then they grounded me. I was only *Colliers*'s number-two correspondent, so I couldn't gain access to areas near the front."

Ernest laughed, turned to Bill Walton. "And I'm their number-one correspondent," he said. "It was Marty who insisted I write for her outfit!" Then he turned back to Martha.

"War coverage is not for women," he said evenly.

She shrugged it off. "They stuck me in an American nurses training camp. But I crawled under the fence and hitched a ride to the next military airport. I told the pilot a very sad story about my fiancé here in Paris whom I simply had to see."

"Oh?" said Ernest. "Why didn't you just say that Mrs. Hemingway wanted to get to Paris so she could celebrate the liberation with her husband, Mr. Hemingway?"

"Because I didn't come to Paris to celebrate with you."

"Then why did you come?"

"To settle a bit of private business with you."

Ernest nodded solemnly, then brightened. "Okay, but not here and now. Come on, have a drink, Marty. Don't be a party-pooper."

Just then an American sergeant stepped up to Ernest, stood at attention, and handed him a piece of paper. "Mr. Hemingway," he said, "I have instructions to bring you to headquarters."

The American Expeditionary Forces headquarters were located in the dining room of a nearby hotel. Colonel Park and two young officers sat at the head of the table, while Ernest, in his war correspondent's uniform, sat in a chair in the middle of the room.

"Mr. Hemingway," said Colonel Park, looking up from his notes, "you are charged with having taken command of the French Resistance forces in Rambouillet."

Ernest held up a finger. "One question before I answer," he said. "What if the charges are proved correct?"

"You will be deprived of your accreditation as a

war correspondent and you will be deported to the United States. But I would like to impress upon you that you are under oath and that perjury is punishable by imprisonment. Mr. Hemingway, did you accept the rank of a colonel in the Resistance movement?"

"No, sir. Ultimately they called me 'colonel' as a courtesy. First they called me 'capitaine,' but then they decided I was too old for a captain."

"How do you explain the arms depot that was found in your hotel room in Rambouillet?"

"Sir, there wasn't enough safe storage area and I was asked to make my room available."

Colonel Park made a note. "Did you have a man with the rank of colonel in the U.S. Army acting as your chief of staff?"

"Sir, I didn't have a staff. The colonel in question requested me to translate his orders into French because I am more familiar with the language—which, by the way, I picked up on the street."

"It has been alleged that you tried to act like one of your fictitious heroes and by doing so impeded the mobility of the fighting units."

A tense silence ensued, one which Ernest seemed to enjoy. Finally, he spoke: "May I suggest, sir, that you have some of your colleagues testify to my character and to my contacts in this area, and that perhaps you begin with Colonel Charles Truman Lanham, Commander of the Twenty-second Regiment, who is currently engaged in combat at the Siegfried Line."

Colonel Park scanned the files lying before him, then clapped them shut. He stood. "Please raise your right hand and repeat after me: I swear that I have told the truth and nothing but the truth so help me God."

"So help me God," said Hemingway.

Back at the Ritz, Ernest went to the reception desk for his key. There he met Mary Welsh, reading her mail.

"Why, hello, Mrs. Mary," he said affably. "What are you doing here?"

She smiled. "I made it! They're letting me cover the victory parade in Paris."

"Congratulations. But don't forget your promise."

"What promise?"

"To celebrate the occasion with me—at the bar."

"Ah," she said, "another time."

"Work?"

Mary nodded. "I have to hurry," she said, turning away. "See you later."

Ernest reached out and took her arm. "I'll see you tonight," he said.

A change came over her. "Where?" she asked.

"My room. Midnight."

"Sounds dangerous."

"We have a lot to talk about, you and me."

"About your wife and my husband?"

"No. About you and me. You must come."

"Why?"

"History demands it."

"Ah," she said, "destiny."

"You'll come?"

"Maybe."

* * *

Bill Walton stopped Ernest on his way to the elevator. Lowering his voice, he asked, "How'd it go? What did they want?"

Ernest shrugged. "The ballroom bananas from SHAEF had a few questions. One of our dear colleagues must have squealed on me because of the Rambouillet stuff. I hope it wasn't you."

Walton laughed. "God forbid, Hem. It probably was that jerk you floored a while back, remember?"

"He's lucky I got to him then. I'd beat the hell out of him if I saw him now."

"How come they let you go?"

"I denied everything and then swore to it. Now the worst thing anybody can call me is a stupid ass."

"Perjury? Congratulations, you stupid ass!"

"We should drink to that," said Hemingway.

Momentarily embarrassed, Walton dropped his eyes. "Uh, sorry, Hem," he said. "I've promised to meet someone."

"Is she nice?"

"Well, yes."

"Who is she? I can keep a secret."

"Well, actually, it's Martha. Your wife."

Amazed, Ernest looked at Walton. Then a big smile spread over his face. He clapped Bill on the shoulder.

"Then, in that case I'll accept your invitation."

* * *

That night a few military officers were having dinner with their wives and girl friends in the Ritz's huge dining room. Ernest, Bill, and Martha sat at a corner table eating quietly, too quietly. Walton tried to change the mood by filling their glasses and proposing a toast.

"Here's to the two of you," he said.

It didn't work. Ernest didn't touch his glass. Martha took a sip, then looked at her husband.

"I think the best thing for us, for me," she said, "is to just call it quits."

Ernest flushed with rage, but managed to control himself. "I hate losing someone who can be as beautiful as you, Marty," he said. "Somebody I've taught to write so well . . . and how to handle a rifle." He turned to Bill, continued in the same vein. "Martha isn't only a great writer, she's also a great hunter. She learned everything from me."

Angry, Martha interrupted. "I was writing books before I ever set eyes on you, Ernest."

He shook his head affably. "Why so ungrateful,

Marty? Go ahead and tell Bill how I taught you to write about war in Madrid."

"That isn't true," she said flatly. "You know I've always gone out of my way not to be simply Mrs. Hemingway. There's nothing wrong with my writing and I don't need you to patronize me. I never did. I know what I can do and so do you."

"Come on," said Walton. "How about a truce?"

Martha paid no attention. She looked at Ernest, her expression full of loathing. "You know as well as I do that our marriage was over long ago. It was a mistake from the very beginning. I want out. Either you let me go without a fight, or I start divorce proceedings on my own."

Ernest threw his napkin in her face. He was on the verge of throwing wine on her dress. "You goddamn bitch!" he thundered. "Someone should tan your hide! But Papa doesn't bear grudges. No—everything's forgiven and forgotten, daughter. You're coming back home with me."

Bill Walton took a deep breath. "Come on, Ernest, stop it. You haven't let up all night."

"You keep out of this!" Ernest screamed.

"I have long enough," answered Walton. "And I've just about had it with your insults."

Martha stood up, and so did Bill. Ernest remained seated. "Sit down, daughter," he ordered. "Do you hear me? I said sit down!"

"Take care, Ernest," she said. "I hope I never have to see you again as long as I live." She turned and strode out of the dining room. Walton ran after her.

Trembling with rage, Ernest stood and screamed after her, "Nobody walks out on me! Nobody! I'm giving you one hundred days to think it over. You hear me, daughter? One hundred days!"

* * *

Pale morning light filtered through the curtains into Ernest's spacious and tastefully decorated room at the Ritz. On the floor were automatic rifles, hand grenades, mines. Also strewn about the floor and furniture were Ernest and Mary's clothes. They lay naked in the large bed, only half covered with a sheet. Ernest lay on his back with Mary's head on his chest. She caressed him tenderly, kissing him everywhere. Suddenly she looked at the clock.

"Oh God, the victory parade! I completely forgot!" She sat up, but Ernest pulled her back. He shook his head.

"Don't go, Mary. There's going to be hundreds of victory parades before the Krauts are finally defeated."

He kissed her. She considered for just a second, then laid her head back down on his chest. She purred like a cat.

"I love you," he said, "and I want you to be my wife."

"You have a wife. And I'm married, too," she answered.

"I had a wife. She left me. The way you'll leave me one day, too. I know. Tell me you don't love me."

She shook her head.

"Then tell me you love me."

"I love you now."

They caressed. "We're so close now," he whispered. "Nothing should ever come between us. You make me feel so strong."

* * *

A few days later Ernest took Mary to the Closerie des Lilas, the cafe where he used to write when he was living in Paris and married to Hadley. He sat at his old table and ordered cafe au lait for Mary, a Rum St. James for himself.

"It's just the way it used to be," he said, looking around.

"What were you writing then?" she asked.

"Short stories. All the men in my stories drank, and then I'd get thirsty, too. I'd always order a Rum St. James. Tasted wonderful on a cold day."

"I wish I'd met you back then. Would you have noticed me?"

"Lots of girls came here, pretty girls that I'd have liked to write into my stories. I used to watch them when I sharpened my pencils."

He looked at her for a moment. When he spoke he sounded as though he were quoting himself. "I saw you, you beauty, and now you belong to me. Even if you're waiting for someone else. You belong to me and all of Paris belongs to me."

"And then?"

"*Up in Michigan*. And then the story was finished and I was damned hungry." He stood, took her hand. "Let's go home," he said.

The next day Louis, Ernest's Jeep driver, took them to the Ile Saint-Louis, where they found a park bench by the Seine. Each of them had a ham sandwich, and there was a bottle of red wine. They watched the fishermen below them. Ernest spoke with a full mouth.

"The best fishing spots change according to the water level. And those are good fish they're catching down there. The best place to eat them was a little cafe called 'La Pêche Miraculeuse,' with a view of the river. It could have been right out of a Maupassant novella or a Sisley painting."

"Were you very happy?"

He nodded. "On nice days I'd buy a liter of wine and some bread and sausage and sit with them in the sun and read books I'd borrowed from Sylvia Beach. I always like coming back to Paris. But it's never the way it was when I was very poor . . . and very happy."

In the afternoon Louis drove them to the Shakespeare & Company bookstore on the rue de l'Odéon, which looked exactly as it did twenty years before. When they entered, Sylvia Beach threw her arms around Ernest's neck.

"I knew you'd come, Ernest. Your exploits are in all the newspapers," she said.

She handed him a copy of *Le Franc Tireur* with photos of himself in the uniform of the Fourth Infantry Division and standing with his Resistance fighters. Ernest scanned it, beaming. Then he introduced Mary.

"Mary, this is Sylvia Beach, an old friend and a friend of writers everywhere, especially American expatriots in Paris. She discovered and published James Joyce's *Ulysses*. Miss Mary is a real devotee of Paris, Sylvia. She's going to be Mrs. Hemingway soon."

"The fourth Mrs. Hemingway! I wish you a good life, Mary. I knew the first Mrs. Hemingway very well. And the second . . . wait a moment." She disappeared into the adjoining office and came back with a small book, a first edition of Hemingway's *Winner Take Nothing*. She opened the book and showed Mary the title page. It was dedicated to herself.

"May I?" Ernest took a gold fountain pen from his pocket, sat down at a table, and under the dedication he wrote, in French,

"Read and approved 26 August, 1944."

* * *

When they returned to the Ritz that night a German singer was standing at the reception desk in a khaki uniform with a knit khaki-colored helmet netting at a slant on her head. Seeing her, Ernest rushed over with wide open arms. She squealed when he picked her off her feet and swung her around.

"Papa!" she cried. "You wonderful, big, beautiful Papa!"

Ernest put her down and beckoned to Mary. "Mary, this is the Kraut! What are you doing here?"

"Trying to keep the American troops in a good mood."

"Come on up to my room and let's have a drink! A bunch of writers are coming and I'm sure we'll have a wild time."

*　*　*

Late that night the get-together party was nearing its close. Empty champagne bottles and glasses were everywhere, canapé remains and full ashtrays, crumpled napkins. The singer stood at the piano in a transparent lamé dress. In her husky voice she sang,

> "Vor der Kaserne, vor dem grossen Tor
> Steht eine laterne und steht sie noch davor
> wenn wir uns dereinst wiederash'n
> werd' ich bei der Laterne steh'n
> wie einst Lili Marleen . . ."

A few young officers, freshly washed with slicked back hair and shiny shoes, were standing stiffly in a corner. They were slightly tipsy, drinking too fast. Mary stood by the door to the bathroom, and she too had had too much to drink. She glanced at Ernest, who was having a wonderful chat with the singer. Ernest called to the officers, waved them over.

To the singer he said, "These are the courageous heroes of the Twenty-second Infantry Regiment. Chased the Krauts back to Krautland the way you drive rats from their holes."

One of the officers whispered something to Ernest, who grinned. "My comrade here has a request," he said to the actress. "He would so like to write home that he'd shared a bed with you."

Without betraying the slightest expression, the chanteuse looked the young man over. Taking him by the hand she led him over to the large double bed. She dropped backward onto the pink satin bedspread and reached out her arms.

The young officer was standing stiffly at attention at the side of the bed. With a heavenly smile he lay down next to her, careful to remain at attention, with his hands pressed up against his trouser seams. Ernest burst into thunderous laughter.

"Hey, Mary! Look at this. The Kraut with her lover in bed!"

Mary turned away. Puzzled, Ernest went to her.

"I'm disgusted," she said.

"With what?"

"The way your friends behave."

"What's wrong with them?"

"Drunkards. They behave like swine."

"Don't talk that way about them," he warned. But she wasn't listening.

"They may be heroes at the front, but here they're pigs."

Unable to control himself, Ernest struck her with the back of his hand, Mary sobered immediately. She rubbed her cheek, looked at Ernest aghast.

"Coward!" she spat. "You think I'm afraid of you?"

Ernest realized he'd gone too far. He tried to soothe her, gloss it over. "You're lovely when you're mad."

"Go on," she said. "Punch me! Go ahead!"

"Okay, take it easy. You've had too much to drink."

She hadn't finished. She nodded to the others, who maintained an embarrassed silence. "Show them how tough Papa is! Papa'll take on any woman. Beat her up good."

Ernest took her hands, but she pulled away. She ran from the room. Ernest took a few steps after her.

"Come back!"

* * *

Mary was sleeping when Ernest entered her room. He stood at the foot of the big double bed and looked down at her lovingly.

"You were absolutely wonderful last night, Pickle," he said.

She awoke, squinted at him. He looked as if he'd been up all night. She was still angry.

"I love you, you cocky lightweight," he said. "You were wonderful, but you don't know how to really hit back. I'm going to teach you."

She sat up, stretched, rubbed her cheek with her hand. "Thanks anyway," she replied. "I've learned enough from you."

He came closer. "You ought to let me show you."

Mary took a deep breath, sniffed. "You need a bath."

"I guess I do. There's a lieutenant asleep in my tub."

"I guess you might as well use mine."

"Mary, I had a bath the day before yesterday."

She pulled up the blankets. "Either you take a hot bath with plenty of soap and all the extras, or you leave!"

* * *

She listened to him in the bathroom. Silence. When she entered he was sitting absolutely still, staring straight ahead.

"Ernest, what are you doing?"

"Huh?" he snapped out of it. "I was thinking."

She picked up the sponge and began to scrub his back. "You drink too much," she said.

"You squawk too much."

"You drink so much you don't know what you're doing."

"Okay. I'll do less drinking, you do less squawking."

"The only reason I squawk is because I don't like drunks. Raise your arms."

"You're right, Pickle. Squawk if you have to. When you squawk I want you more than anybody I ever knew."

"And your wives? What about Martha? What about Pauline? In fact, you're a fool not to go back to them."

"Both of them?"

"Put your arms down and be serious. You should go back to Martha."

"Can't. We've done too many horrible things to each other."

"You could write to her and ask forgiveness."

"Mary," he said at length, "there are some things I just can't explain to you while I'm in the tub."

Ernest got out of the tub and Mary wrapped him with a big white Ritz bath towel. He put his arms around her and squeezed. "You're wonderful and beautiful and it keeps dawning on me how much I love you and need you and always will love you and need you."

"Always bullshit!"

"Truth!"

"Are you ever going to grow up, Ernest Hemingway?"

He laughed, spanked her bottom. "Only if you ever decide to marry me!"

Havana—Spring, Summer 1946

The lawyer's office was a spacious dark room in an old building near the port. It was hot and the single ceiling fan turned so slowly it barely disturbed the air. Ernest and Mary, sitting in old wooden chairs, listened carefully while the lawyer, in a rattling voice, read the appropriate passages about property rights and the marriage contract from the Code Napoléon, in Spanish. They reached the part which says that in the case of divorce all gifts exchanged between the two parties must be returned.

Mary looked at her engagement ring, then at Ernest. "I'd have to give this back, too?"

Ernest and the lawyer nodded.

"And what do I get from you?"

"Everything I own," Ernest replied.

The lawyer came to an end. He spread the papers, already drawn up, for them to sign. He dipped a quill in an ink well and handed it to Ernest. He signed, then Mary. The lawyer came from behind his desk to congratulate the newlyweds.

Ernest took Mary in his arms and kissed her. "This calls for a cup of hemlock," he said.

Late that summer Ernest was lying in the shade of a thatch baldachin next to the swimming pool at the Finca Vigia, playing with his cat, Boise. Boise lay on his back, all four feet in the air, while Ernest stroked his stomach.

"You're feeling fine now, aren't you, Boise?"

The cat purred.

"You have a new mistress now, huh? And she's really nice to you. Not like the other one who just wanted to cut off your balls."

Mary came out on the veranda. She ran down the steps and over to Ernest, and sat down next to him. She was wearing maternity clothes and beaming.

"Papa?"

"What's up, daughter?"

"Ernest, you always wanted a daughter."

He nearly fell over into the pool. He sat up.

"Are you sure?"

"The doctor said there's no doubt."

A wide grin spread across his face. "She'll have your figure, Pickle. Your legs, your breasts."

"Your eyes!"

"No, your eyes. And your hair, your lips, your nose and ears."

"But your brain."

"Impossible. She'd be boring if she had my brains and was as pretty as you are."

She laughed. "Little babies are never boring."

"Nothing dumber than babies," he said, shaking his head. "The main thing is that she has a good governess and isn't pampered."

Mary laid her head on his chest and caressed him. He looked at her questioningly. "You're still coming, aren't you?"

"Where?

"Sun Valley. The boys really want you to come along. They're dying to meet you."

"All right, I'll come," she said.

"Thank God. For a second I thought you were going to let the baby make you crazy."

"Why should I?"

"It happens, believe me. And once it happens everything really goes to hell. Including the baby."

She pushed him into the pool.

En Route to Sun Valley—Winter, 1946

The ambulance was parked with its doors open in the front of the motel, next to Ernest's Lincoln. A few curious guests in their bathrobes were standing in doorways, watching. Two orderlies carried Mary on a stretcher to the ambulance. Unconscious, her face pale, she was wrapped in a pink blanket. Holding her hand, Ernest walked alongside.

"She's in her second month," he told the orderlies. "She's thirty-eight. It's her first pregnancy, you see."

They nodded and pushed the stretcher into the ambulance.

"We've been traveling hard for two weeks," he continued. "Everything was just fine until this morning. She woke up screaming—with stomachaches. She lost consciousness while I was calling the hospital."

The orderlies closed the ambulance doors and asked Ernest to follow them to the hospital. Ernest got behind the wheel of the Lincoln. His hands were shaking so hard he could not put the key in the switch.

Taking a deep breath, he calmed himself, started the car.

* * *

Mary lay on the operating table. Two nurses checked her plasma bottles, shaking their heads. A young physician washed his hands under running water, then let a nurse help him put on rubber gloves.

Ernest watched through a little window to the operating room. He turned to the nurse at his side. "This assistant physician," he said. "Is he the only doctor in the hospital?"

The nurse nodded. "It's a small hospital."

"Where's the resident physician?"

"Fishing."

"Well, can't he be reached?"

"We don't know where he is," she replied. "We've tried. Don't worry, Mr. Hemingway. We'll do everything we can for your wife."

She took his arm and led him out into the hallway to a couch. "Stay here and we'll let you know exactly how she is, all right?"

* * *

Hours later the assistant physician appeared in the corridor. He looked exhausted and depressed, his surgeon's mask dangling limply from his neck. He pulled off his gloves.

"Tubal pregnancy," he said. "A rupture of the Fallopian tube. Heavy internal bleeding."

"What are you doing for her?" Red-eyed and exhausted, Ernest stood, towering over the young doctor.

"We gave her a spinal. Then her circulatory system collapsed. No pulse. We can't get a needle in her vein to administer plasma. It's hopeless. It's impossible to operate."

"Is she dead?" Ernest asked.

The doctor shook his head.

"Doc, she's been lying in there twelve hours."

"Her veins have collapsed. I can't get a needle in. It's hopeless."

"Nothing is hopeless, not as long as there's life."

The doctor shrugged. "Would you like to go in and have a few last words with her? She's unconscious."

"How am I supposed to have a few last words with her if she's unconscious?"

"I'm sorry."

Ernest looked at the physician. Then he walked past him into the operating room.

"Doctor," he said, "my wife is not going to die. Would you come with me, please?"

Shaking his head, the doctor followed.

Mary lay on the operating table as she had that morning, pale and lifeless. Ernest put on a smock, a mask and gloves. Looking like a surgeon, he said to the doctor and the nurses, "Okay. We're going to give fate a boot in the ass. Make an incision," he directed. "Open up a vein."

They stood around staring at him. Nobody moved. Ernest remained calm, but there was no mistaking his voice of authority.

"Doctor," he said. "I'd like you to open up a vein, please."

The assistant physician hesitated for a second, then nodded to one of the nurses. She handed him a scalpel. The doctor bent over Mary and made the incision. Ernest inspected the plasma tubes.

"This valve isn't opened far enough," he said. "The plasma has to flow freely." He twisted the valve.

Holding Mary's arm, Ernest handed the physician the plastic cannulas. He slid them into the open vein and waited. Mary's face was pale. Ernest stared at the oscillograph, which should have been registering a heartbeat. The point moved from left to right, but only slightly. With soft steady motions Ernest pumped the plasma into her arms. Suddenly the point jumped, moved farther. Mary began to breathe, at first almost imperceptibly, then stronger and stronger. Then, miraculously, her eyes opened.

"Hello, Mary," said Ernest Hemingway.

Cuba—Summer, 1947

A sunny summer day, still cool in morning. Ernest drove the white Lincoln convertible down a country road, watching the scenery. At his side, Mary regarded her pale face in the rearview mirror. She frowned.

"A Distinguished Service Cross with an ETO ribbon is the very least I deserve, wouldn't you say?" he joked. "But I guess the Bronze Star's better than nothing, huh?"

She forced a smile. He tried to cheer her. "Just wait, Pickle. When they see you, their eyes'll pop out. Everybody's dressed to the hilt and look at me." He looked down at his dirty white shirt hanging outside his pants. He laughed, then looked at Mary. There were tears in her eyes.

"You're still sad about the baby," he said.

"Oh, Ernest, I wanted her so badly for you."

"Well, we'll just try again, that's all."

She shook her head forlornly. "You know there's no trying again. Stop the car!"

He brought the Lincoln to a halt. She put her arms

around his neck. "I needed a hug," she said. He hugged her, hard.

"Papa, I promise you that I will never, ever forget what you did for me."

A short time later they arrived at their destination, the United States Embassy, in Havana, where Ernest was to be honored for his war efforts. His white cotton shirt was still untucked as he stood before the Stars and Stripes, facng the elegantly dressed officials. The U.S. Ambassador fixed a medal, the Bronze Star, to his shirt.

". . . as a reporter in France and Germany, where he illustrated extensive knowledge of modern warfare, interpreting and evaluating battles and operations of our own forces as well as those of the enemy, and where he moved freely and at great personal risk through areas of combat to obtain an accurate picture of the situation."

The Ambassador took a step back. He came to attention and saluted. Ernest came to attention and saluted. He was deeply moved. Afterwards, drinks were passed around and a few reporters appeared at Ernest's side.

"Mr Hemingway," said one, "do you actually like war?"

"I hate war."

"After the war," began another, "the United States emerged as the most powerful country in the world. Do you—"

Ernest interrupted him, "It's important that the U.S. doesn't become the most hated country in the world," he said.

He was asked to explain his remark.

"The American forces performed great deeds," he said. "But they probably killed more civilians than our enemy did in all the massacres we find so outrageous."

"Are you referring to the atom bomb?"

"The atom bomb is the sling and the stone that

can annihilate all giants, including the United Nations. We in America mustn't tolerate even the slightest trace of Fascist thinking."

"Do you mean Senator McCarthy?"

Ernest evaded a direct reference. "I mean we must not become hypocritical, sanctimonious, and vengeful," he stated. "That would be a mistake. We must learn not to tamper with other countries' rights, privileges, and obligations."

The reporters were zeroing in. "Does that also hold true for the American forces here in Cuba?"

Ernest's searching eyes found Mary. He nodded and she moved over to him, pulled him away from the reporters with an obliging laugh. When they were alone, Ernest took a deep breath.

"Why didn't you help me sooner?"

She kissed him. "It's your show and I think you handled it very well."

"Come on," he said, looking for an exit. "Let's get out of here."

That night they found their way to their usual spot at the L-shaped counter of the Floridita Bar. Sitting around them were a few locals, expatriots, Cubans, sailors, and a somewhat heavyset whore. Ernest played with his bronze star as though it were a coin. He was drunk, slightly aggressive, and alert.

"They gave me the bronze star," he expounded. "I really deserved the Distinguished Service Cross for the rat race through France. Drove the Krauts all over hell! Took prisoners. No time for being sentimental. I shot a German officer standing as close to me as you are." He leaned toward the whore and poked her fat stomach with his forefinger. Mary winced.

"The arrogant sonofabitch," Ernest continued. "I couldn't stand him. Warned him I'd shoot him if he didn't talk."

He stood and began acting out his story. "He told me I wouldn't kill him because I was afraid. I asked him why should I be afraid. He said because I belonged to a morally degenerated bastard race!"

He held his medal over his upper lip, and with his left hand he performed a Heil-Hitler salute. Everyone laughed. Ernest couldn't stop.

"I told him he was sorely mistaken." Ernest poked the whore in her stomach again. She giggled, gave a painful little jerk. Disgusted, Mary turned away. Ernest put his forefinger to the whore's head, held his hand like a pistol.

"*Bam, bam, bam!* I shot him three times in the gut and finished him with one in the head! His brains spilled out on the floor." Ernest's glass was empty. He signaled for another daiquiri.

Mary got up. She watched with revulsion as the whore started to caress Ernest's stomach. Ernest whispered something in her ear. She laughed heartily, spilling her drink.

When Ernest looked back to Mary she was gone.

The sun was rising when he went to her. She was asleep in their bedroom, a small shape in the huge bed. He sat beside her, put his hand on her cheek. She woke, looked at him, and smiled. But quickly the smile disappeared.

"I'm sorry," he said.

She lowered her head passively.

"Don't be mad at me, Pickle."

Silence.

Ernest got up and paced the room. "Why do I always have to make up such stupid stories? There's no reason why I have to lie about what I did in the war. I hate myself when I go on like that. I'm a braggart, blowhard, big mouth!"

"Ernest," she said at last, "your boasting and lying and the way you feel afterwards—those are your problems, not mine. But when you try to humiliate me—"

He wouldn't let her continue. "The war wrecked

me," he said, sitting next to her again. "Too much brutality, too much alcohol, too uncivilized. Everything's dead inside, Mary. I haven't written anything in six years. I don't want to live this way. Writing kills me, but if I don't write—oh Christ, I can't live without it!" He pressed his hands to his temples.

"What's the matter?" she said, sitting up.

"Pounding in my head. Very delicate instrument. I've got to try to get my thinking machine back on the right track."

"Too many concussions, dear. You have to try to forget the war."

"I don't want to forget the war. I don't want to forget anything. I need this war the way I needed the Spanish Civil War and World War I. I've got to go back. Mary, we'll go to Europe and I'll write again like I used to, I swear. I'll write a book just for you and I'll dedicate it to you."

"With love?"

Ernest laughed. "Well, I've never done that before, but I will this time."

Ernest looked at Mary with fear and panic in his eyes. He hugged her tightly. Mary was crying. He stroked her hair with one hand. She snuggled up to him like a child.

"I'll never leave you," she said. "Not unless you tell me to."

Italy—Winter, 1948

The old and battered taxi came up the paved road by the dike and wound through a soft S-curve which allowed a spectacular view of the bend in the river, the church steeple and the houses of Fossalta, where the Italians had dug in thirty years before. On the left side, below the dike, was an aspen wood. The trees had been planted symmetrically so that they formed a fascinating graphic pattern in the foggy morning.

Ernest tapped the taxi driver on the shoulder, told him to stop. The car pulled up to the edge of the dike. Ernest and Mary got out. They held hands and looked down at the river. Ernest pointed to a cultivated field.

"That's where I got hit," he said. "You know, my mother never forgave me for coming back from World War I alive."

At a loss, Mary asked him what he meant.

"I cheated her out of becoming a Gold Star mother."

"Ernest, you're insensitive and crude."

"Look down there, Pickle. That's where I realized what it's all about. Just one thing: learning to live with death without being afraid, and to die when the time comes. Nobody is really free until they're ready to live with their own death."

"But you were just a boy."

"Two weeks shy of my nineteenth birthday. I volunteered. Too bad. There's been no more of the go-getter in me since that day."

"It changed your life?"

He nodded. "You only feel true tenderness and love for those who were there and went through the same sort of thing. Oh, the hell with it." Suddenly he ran down the embankment.

"Where are you going?" Mary called.

"To erect myself a monument!"

She watched from above as he moved around in a thicket, apparently looking for something. Finally, he stopped.

"It must have been right around here!" he shouted. From his pocket he took a 10,000 lire note. He dug a hole in the moist earth with his hands and put the bill in, covered it up. He padded down the earth with his foot, laughed, then ran back up the hill.

"A feeble attempt, Mary, but my very own," he said. "Now it's all there—money, blood, and guts. And Gino's leg, and my right kneecap. An infernal little patch of earth. The grass will be incredibly lush."

They were in Venice three days when a letter arrived by messenger. Ernest tore it open and read it in their hotel room.

"It's an invitation to go duck hunting, Mary. Baron Franchetti says he'd be honored if we would be his guests."

"But we're leaving soon for Florence," she said.

"We can postpone it, huh?"

"I'm so looking forward to Florence."

"I'm not here as a tourist, Pickle."

"You're here as a duck hunter?"

"As a writer."

"Okay," she said, giving in. "If that's what you want, go ahead. But do you mind if I don't join you? I'm sure the baron will understand if I take a look at the museums instead."

*   *   *

The flat, gondolalike boats glided over the velvety water. In the sterns of the boats the punters pushed along the bottom with their long poles. The hunters sat on small stools in the middle of the boats. In the bows the dogs waited.

Ernest sat next to the baron. They put out wooden decoys, checked their guns. Ernest kept looking at one of the other boats, where a slim, dark-haired, pretty girl sat facing the stern. She had a thin, pale face with hazel eyes shaded by her prominent cheekbones and a slightly curved, aristocratic nose. She held a sketch pad on her knee, and with light strokes of her pencil she drew the hunting party. With the exception of herself, it was entirely male.

"The ducks fly down from the north," said Baron Franchetti. "There are many big ones of the very best kind. There is nothing better to eat than these ducks from behind the iron curtain. They come down over the large fields of grain in the Ukraine and along the Danube. Large ducks with gray heads, superb ducks, fat as pigs, heavy with the stuff they ate in Russia."

A few live ducks were removed from sacks and put into the water, where they began quacking and calling excitedly. A flock of pintails dived down to them. Ernest swung his shotgun in a long arc and fired. Everyone fired.

Ernest was distracted by a short cry from the pretty girl. While swinging his gun in the direction of the flock, one of the hunters had hit her forehead with the stock. She flinched, but was all right. Ernest kept his eye on her.

Following his gaze, the baron nodded. "That is Countess Adriana. She comes from a very distinguished Venetian family," he said.

"She's hurt."

"Not seriously."

"She's very beautiful."

"She is nineteen years old, my friend. Her parents' house was magnificent. It was destroyed by the Americans."

* * *

The small room in the hunting lodge had a stone floor, heavy, old furniture, a shiny, worn table, and two large armoires. Most of the light came from a fire burning in a small stove in one corner. Adriana knelt before it, trying to dry her hair. She could hear the hunters' voices in the adjoining room, talking, laughing, retelling the hunt. Suddenly she sensed she was not alone. Standing in the doorway, a bottle of Chianti in one hand, was Ernest.

"May I come in?" he asked.

"Please," she said, "Signor Hemingway."

He went to her and produced two glasses he'd

been holding behind his back. "A little *russo?*" he asked.

"No, *grazie*."

He pointed to the small but deep wound on her forehead. "Does it hurt?" he asked.

"Excuse me, my English is not very well."

"Here," he said, moving closer, "let me take a look."

He took her head in his hands, turned it a bit to the side so that the firelight fell on the wound. He shook his head. "It's not bad."

She nodded, looking up at him. He felt her damp hair.

"May I help?" he asked. Again she nodded, handing him the towel. Very tenderly he began to rub her hair.

"Tell me if I'm too rough."

She stared at him.

"I'm told your house was destroyed by the Americans," he said. "I'm sorry. I hope you've forgiven us."

"War is war," she said. "No one can be blamed."

"God damn war! Excuse the expression."

She looked at him. "My friends say you are a very great writer. But I have not read one of your books."

He nodded. "My books weren't even sold in Italy until after the war. So you don't have to apologize. You won't learn anything of value from my books, anyway."

"If you look," said Adriana simply, "you can find something of value everywhere."

Ernest did not answer. He gave his full attention to her hair.

"Forgive me," she said. "What I said was silly— *stupido*."

He shook his head. "Not at all. What you say is true. Say, when I was watching you today—and I was watching you—you were sketching. May I see what you've done?"

She got her sketch pad and handed it to him. The

drawings were excellent, her talent was obvious. Hemingway was delighted.

"This one, with the long nose, it's Carlo, huh? And this one. Uh oh. The big belly. A certain Hemingstein from Michigan? He could stand to lose a few pounds."

Embarrassed, Adriana looked down. Ernest laughed.

"Would you mind if I called you 'daughter'?"

"No."

"Your hair is beautiful. Do you have a comb?"

She shook her head. Ernest fetched a comb from his bag, broke it in two, and handed her half of it.

"*Grazie*, Papa," she said, laughing.

"I'd like to see you again. Do you have time?"

* * *

The morning sun was cold on the Grand Canal. A page boy dressed in Gritti Palace Hotel livery crossed the canal in a gondola. He was singing.

"*Tutti mi chiamo bionda . . .*"

He climbed ashore carrying a shopping basket full of bottles. Crossing the small square before the hotel, he disappeared in the entrance reserved for personnel.

On the third floor, standing in an open, arched window, was Mary. She turned to Ernest, who was lying on the bed.

"I hope you didn't invite her here for lunch," she said.

Ernest looked up from his notes. "No, she's going to call me as soon as she gets up," he replied.

The expansive hotel room was typically Venetian. The walls were covered with embroidered silk tapestries. A full candelabrum hung from the ceiling. Four huge mirrors were framed by electric rococo crystal lamps. It was very disorderly. Luggage was everywhere, boxes, suitcases half-unpacked, books, newspapers, magazines, writing paper, empty bottles.

Mary returned to her chair by the window. She

was embroidering Ernest's monogram onto a heavy terrycloth bathrobe while he wrote.

"You don't think you're seeing her a little too often?" she said. "I just wonder what her mother thinks."

Ernest was lying in bed, wearing a trench coat over his pajamas. Strewn about him were manuscript pages, paper, books, pencils, a small dictionary. On the table beside the bed was a half-empty bottle of champagne and Ernest's empty glass. He looked up.

"What does her mother think?" he asked sarcastically.

"Do you think it's proper for a young school girl to keep meeting a famous writer in bars and cafes—a writer who's not only known all over the city and is so much older than she, but also happens to be married? People are going to talk."

Ernest shrugged. "Hey, I couldn't care less," he said. "In Venice there are no secrets anyway. Besides, everybody knows her family and everybody knows she's a nice girl."

"And what does everybody know about you?"

"You're jealous," he said, sitting up. "You don't like my being with her. You don't like it because when I'm with her I feel young and happy."

Just then there was a knock at the door. Mary opened it and in swept Mario, the hotel page boy, carrying the basket of bottles. A draft blew all the loose papers about, but neither Mary nor Ernest bothered to pick them up. Mario placed the bottles—gin, Scotch, vodka, and champagne—on a table and collected the empty bottles.

Ernest gave him a tip and asked him to repeat the song he'd been singing in the gondola. The boy sang the words and Ernest recalled them from long before, a song popular in the Italian army ranks. He sang along.

"Tutti mi chiamo bionda . . ."

When the song was over Mario bowed and left the

room. As he did so another draft blew the rest of the papers from the table. Mary ignored them. Finished with her embroidery, she stood and handed it to Ernest. He tried it on, standing before a mirror. He tied the belt and shifted his shoulders to check the fit. When the telephone rang he grabbed it.

"Hello, daughter. Yes. How'd you sleep? Good. Of course we can, whenever and wherever you like. How about breakfast at Florian's on the piazza? Fine. I'll be there in twenty minutes. Okay, see you soon, daughter."

Mary looked at Ernest with a bitter expression on her face. "You always wanted a daughter," she said.

"Don't start that again," he said with a sigh.

"You've never forgiven me," she said, holding back a sob. "But even if it had worked out, you'd have had to wait nineteen years before you had a daughter like Adriana."

"Stop it, please, Mary. The one thing has nothing to do with the other." He was busy dressing, rushing.

"You must think I'm a fool," she said.

He went to her, lifted her chin. "Is it a crime to love two women at the same time?"

She pulled herself away. "How little you know about yourself," she said ruefully. "Sure, just dream on. You've thrown out your nets and you don't even realize that you're the one who's all tangled up. I'll go to Florence alone."

Ernest nodded matter-of-factly. "How long will you stay?"

"A few weeks."

"That's a long time."

She shook her head. "I don't want to have to watch you hurt yourself," she said.

* * *

There were only a few customers at the Cafe Florian, reading newspapers and sipping cappuccino.

Ernest sat at a corner looking out over the empty square. A happy smile spread across his face when he spotted Adriana hurrying to the cafe. Out of breath, she gave Ernest a kiss on the cheek. He helped her out of her coat, gave it to the waiter.

"This young lady would like a breakfast to end all breakfasts," he said with a wink.

"May I suggest an omelet with truffles that were excavated by very distinguished pigs?"

"Va bene."

"With some imported Canadian bacon?"

"Very good," said Ernest. "And for me, a bottle of Valpolicella, and a little bacon. Oh hell, plenty of bacon."

The waiter sped away. Ernest turned to Adriana, his smile never leaving his face.

"And how are you, dear?" he said, taking her hand.

"Very hungry."

"A young girl should always be so. What do you say to a little excursion after breakfast?"

"If you like, Papa."

"How about Torcello? I want to look at a couple of rooms in the Locando."

"Fine."

He gave her hand a squeeze. "Mary is going to Florence for a few weeks. I might move over to the Locando. If we take a taxi we'll be there in twenty minutes."

"I must tell my mother."

"Absolutely," he said. "You should call home and ask your parents' permission."

"No, I'm not going to ask their permission."

"No?"

She laughed. "I'm just going to tell them."

* * *

The motorboat-taxi glided smoothly over the water, in its wake a cloud of spray in the pale clear sun. Ernest and Adriana stood exposed to the wind on the small deck behind the cabin. Adriana almost had to shout to make herself heard. She pointed to their destination, the island of Torcello.

"The people who lived there were chased from the mainland by the Visigoths," she explained. "They constructed the church with the square tower. They were thirty thousand. And then the malaria came. When it was over, the survivors tore down their homes. They put the stones in boats and came back here and built Venice."

The boat went down a narrow side canal and moored by a small stone bridge diagonally across from the famous Locando hotel. Ernest helped Adriana out of the boat. He looked around and took a deep breath.

"This is where I'll work," he said.

"May I come and visit you?" she asked demurely.

"I couldn't work if you didn't."

"But it might not be proper."

He took her hand. "Let's look at the rooms, daughter."

They entered the hotel, taking the narrow stone staircase to the second floor. The proprietor showed them a room. It was small and comfortable, with a big bed and a carved marble fireplace. Ernest went to the window, opened it, and looked out at the massive Roman basilica.

"I'll take it," he said.

* * *

A few days later Ernest was sitting at one of the wicker tables in the hotel garden, alone and writing. He read aloud his last paragraph.

Hemingway had transformed Adriana's history of Torcello into moving sentences relating the story of the island in the lagoon. As he read his voice was level. The stones of the garden glowed warmly in the sun. Across from him the canal waters were an intense blue, darker than the open waters of the lagoon. A small black kitten sat in the shade, gazing at him with approval, he thought, of the work he had just done.

He looked up and saw Adriana standing in a doorway, watching him. He smiled, put down his pencil, waved to her.

"Seeing you is like opening a bottle of champagne," he said.

"I don't want to disturb you while you work, Papa."

"Ha! You're not disturbing me. I'm just about finished for today, anyway. Three hundred and eighty words are enough."

"You count the words you write?"

"An old habit I picked up as a journalist."

"And you are making good *progresso?*"

He nodded solemnly. "I wish I could show you something," he said. "A painter can show his picture. A dancer can do his dance. But a writer? All he has to show for a morning's work is a piece of paper or two. Nobody's impressed."

"What is it about?"

"About getting old and dying. War and love."

"A sad story?"

"Sad and not sad at the same time. It's about all the new and astounding things that life constantly offers. How you have to be amazed and grateful and prepared to accept them without despair, right up to the end."

"Is there anything you'd like to do, to see?" she asked.

"How about the church tower?"

"Of course!" she said. "Come, I know where they hide the key."

They walked past the baptistery, through the stone

gate and along the basilica to the tower. While they walked they discussed the plot and characters of Ernest's new book. She was puzzled.

"It's impossible," she said. "If the girl is so beautiful, if she comes from a good family, goes to mass every morning, then she couldn't do the things you say she does."

"Like what?"

"A girl like that would never spend the whole day drinking with the colonel. She wouldn't lie around in hotel rooms, and she wouldn't make love in a gondola."

"You're mistaken, Adriana," he said. "There are girls like that."

"In America maybe. Not here in Venezia."

Ernest stopped, looked at her seriously. "Listen, Adriana," he said. "Maybe you don't understand. Maybe you're too young. This book isn't about living people. The characters are invented. They live in my head. You're not Roberta and I'm not the colonel who dies in the car."

When he moved on, she followed. Ernest opened the door to the tower, held it while she passed through. They climbed the winding passageway, round and round the interior of the square tower, until they reached the top. Ernest, a little winded, was cocky, in high spirits. He was playing at being the youthful, fresh, strong man.

"I'm going to blow all the critics away with this one, daughter! I'll show 'em who's champ. I'll knock Mr. Tolstoy out! Maybe I've already sent Mr. Turgenev to the mat. It only took four of my best short stories to knock out Mr. Maupassant, and I took care of Mr. Henry James with my bare thumb!"

"And is there anyone you cannot beat?" she asked.

"Mr. Shakespeare. He's the all-time champion. You have to have confidence in yourself if you want to be champ, and that's the only thing I've ever wanted. I've got all the confidence in the world, but I know my name will never be mentioned in the same sentence with William Shakespeare's. It doesn't bother me."

Suddenly Ernest stopped still. He looked at Adriana. There was something desperate in his expression. A light breeze moved her hair. He touched her cheek. She was concerned.

"What is it?" she asked. "What's wrong?"

He put his arms around her and kissed her. Shocked, she pulled away, looked at him, then at the lagoon. She did not dare look at Ernest as he whispered in her ear.

"Adriana," he said plaintively, "I love you and I can't help it."

"But you have Mary."

"Sure, Mary. She's a good pal. But you, I love you with all my heart. I want the best for you. I know what you need . . . to be happy. I'd beg you to marry me if I didn't know you'd turn me down."

Gondolas crossed the lagoon, taking tourists to and from the mainland. Adriana watched them, showing no emotion. When she spoke it was only to announce that it was time to go.

Cuba—Summer, 1948

It was a balmy morning and Mary's garden was in full bloom. The golden yellow nasturtium was growing wildly under a ceiba tree, and the frangipani, the bougainvillea, the paulownia and jasmine were fragrant and full of blossoms.

Ernest went to the mailbox and returned with a small package. He was wearing shorts and a white cotton sweatshirt. He looked pleased with himself as he opened the package. Mary was setting the coffee table, and without a word, Ernest handed her the first copy of *Across the River and Into the Trees*.

"Open it," he said. "It's dedicated to you."

Mary opened it. "To Mary with love," she read, making a face. She snapped it shut, put it down next to her plate.

Ernest stared at her. "Aren't you happy? I dedicated a book to you, as I promised, and you're frowning. What's up?"

"What am I supposed to make of it? You dedicate it to me with love—while the heroine of the book is your little Venetian countess."

"Leave Adriana out of this, Mary. It's a novel, it has nothing to do with her."

"The only reason you did it is because you hate me."

"Why should I hate you?"

"You blame me because you didn't get her."

"Be quiet," said Ernest menacingly. "I'm warning you."

She narrowed her eyes. "I don't have to put up with your threats."

"You should take a look in the mirror, Mary. You look like Torquemada. The Grand Inquisitor in person."

"*You* take a look at yourself," she replied. "Your moods, your depressions. You drink like a fish. It makes me sick the way you hang around with your whores every night in the Floridita bar. Sick!"

"Mary, as long as I'm writing well that's my business. This is the best book I've ever written, that *anyone's* ever written. I'm going to kick Shakespeare's ass with this one!"

"Oh yes, Papa's the greatest," she said, her voice dripping with sarcasm. "He's so great he doesn't even notice when he starts parodying himself. You know what you are? You're the groggy champ hanging on to the ropes."

Ernest could control himself no longer. He jumped up, knocking over a chair. He screamed at Mary.

"If you don't like it get out! Go back to your parents!"

"Okay," she said, "I will. Just don't start whimpering and come crawling back to me when I'm gone."

He laughed, but it was false. "You won't leave me! You're not even capable of that."

Mary stood up. Crying, she ran into the house.

"I've had it!" he shouted at her. "I can't stand the sight of you! Your constant bitching makes me sick! I want you out of here by the time I get back!"

Half an hour later Ernest was sitting at his usual spot in the Floridita. Around him were a few whores and fishermen friends he was treating to drinks. Slowly, but without interruption, he emptied his glass. The bartender whipped him up another daiquiri.

One of his friends held up the *New York Times Book Review*. "Hey, Ernest. Says here you're the best writer since Shakespeare."

Ernest nodded solemnly. "Dr. Shakespeare might've met some people I didn't meet, but I know all sorts of prizefighters, painters, diplomats, thieves, gangsters, politicians, jockeys, roughriders, bullfighters."

He put his arm around the girl next to him. "And ladies too. Beautiful women, great ladies. And plenty of hired killers, all kinds of gamblers, anarchists, socialists, democrats, communists!"

Everyone in the bar was listening, waiting. Ernest downed his daiquiri and continued his rambling discourse.

"Battalions of barflies! And a chaplain in the army lent me money and I went bordello hopping and wrote during the day, and I paid him back! It's just a pile of crap anyway. And then this bull about how the women in my books don't really exist!"

He directed his question to the woman beside him. "Do you believe that? What those maggot critics mean is that they've never met women like mine! Right? Am I right?"

* * *

That night Ernest loaded the Lincoln with his drinking friends and drove home to the finca. Mary was waiting on the veranda, dressed as she had been that morning. Ernest walked up the steps with a whore on either arm. He smiled.

"Hey, Mary, we got visitors!" he said drunkenly. "Aren't you going to say hello? Look, this here is Xenophobia and this is Leopoldina. Ladies, this is my wife, Mary. Don't you want to get changed, Mary? And how about something to eat? We're starved!"

They walked past Mary into the house.

They sat at the big round table in the dining room, passing a bottle of rum from hand to hand. Cats were everywhere, running and fighting under the table. Leopoldina sat on Ernest's lap, one arm around his neck. With her other hand she reached into his shirt and started scratching his hairy chest.

Mary appeared, changed, and carrying a large platter of sandwiches. She put it on the table. Amidst laughter from everyone, Ernest took the platter and set it on the floor, then started passing out sandwiches to the cats.

"All the countesses in Venice had the hots for me! Isn't that right, Mary? Go on, tell them!"

"Yes," said Mary softly. "All the women wanted to go to bed with Papa."

"Hell, once I did it in a gondola under an army blanket on a windy canal!!" He whispered into Leopoldina's ear: "Ever do it in a gondola?"

She burst out in shrieks of laughter. She ran her hand through his white, thinning hair. Suddenly Ernest turned red. He jumped up, dumping the girl onto the floor.

"Don't ever do that with me!" he shouted. "Nobody touches my head!"

His friends stared at him. He exploded. "All right, get out!" he screamed. "All of you, get out!"

They scampered from the house, stumbling down the garden path. Ernest threw their hats and jackets after them.

Mary was sitting quietly on the veranda, stroking a cat. He sat on a step near her, put his head in his hands.

"I'm sorry, Kitten," he said.

Mary nodded. "I know how unhappy you are, Ernest. Do you remember what I told you in Venice? You're hurting yourself most of all. Stop tormenting yourself. I promised you I wouldn't leave."

Hemingway stared into the dark evening. "Adriana was fresh," he said quietly. "She was like a fir tree in snow way up in the mountains. She was exciting, like a good gun, and she was beautiful. She was so beautiful that when I dreamed about her I woke up stronger than the day before, and the words just flowed out of me."

Mary was impervious, used to it by now. "That's over now," she said. "It's behind you. Be happy."

But Ernest began to cry.

"This morning I took the *Pilar* out," he said between sobs. "Way, way out where it's two thousand meters deep. I dove into the water and swam down until I couldn't go any further, then I slowly let my breath out. It was so easy. All I had to do was breathe in the water and I never would have come back to the surface."

She looked at her husband sadly. Pushing the cat from her lap, she got up, went over and sat down next to him. "Come in now, Papa," she said.

"You didn't really mean that, did you?" he asked. "What?"

"What you said this morning, that I'm groggy . . ."

"No, of course I didn't mean it. You just had to write her out of your system. Now you'll find your way back to the old stories, don't worry."

He nodded. "Yes, I'll write a good book. I swear it, Mary. Better than anything I've written yet. It's a story I've been carrying around in my head for fifteen years. Want to hear it?"

"Of course."

"It's the story of an old Cuban fisherman and his fight with a huge swordfish."

"Does he win the fight?"

"I'm not sure."

* * *

The following day Ernest was awake early, standing at his writing desk, pencil in hand. He was concentrating when Mary came in with a telegram.

"Later," he said. "This is really going well."

"Ernest, it's from your sister, Sunny."

He stopped writing, looked at her.

"Your mother, Ernest. She died yesterday. In the hospital in Memphis."

He turned away and began to write.

"Did you hear me?" she asked, concerned.

"I'm not deaf."

"Is that all you have to say? Ernest, she was your mother."

"Yes, she was my mother. I used to love her. But that was before she started being horrid to my father. Now I hate her. And she hated me."

"That's not true. Don't you remember, just recently, she wrote how much she loved you?"

"A lie," he said. "You know very well that she drove my father to suicide. She gave me his revolver so I could kill myself, too."

"I thought you asked her for it."

There was no reply.

Africa—Winter, 1954

The small Cessna 180 was parked on a provisional landing strip near their camp. Ernest, Mary, and the other members of the safari sat on the ground by a thorny bush that was decorated with lit candles. On the radio German Christmas carols were playing. It was Christmas day and Mary passed out small gifts to the safari helpers. To Ernest she gave a small bag. From it he pulled two pairs of dark brown, shining boxing gloves. He gave her a kiss on the mouth, thrilled.

Hooting and laughing, he put on the gloves and handed the other pair to a young black scout. Wearing his bush shirt with a woolen beanie on his head, his pants tucked into knee-high riding boots, Ernest began to spar. His enjoyment was innocent and youthful. He used his repertoire of feints, hooks, and uppercuts, but neither of them tried to hit very hard.

When the match was over, he went to the dining tent and sat down with Mary and Roy Marsh, the pilot of the Cessna. Mary unlaced his gloves.

"A wonderful Christmas present, Kitten," he said. "And now, here's my present to you." He opened a map and ran his finger over it.

"We're going to fly over the Serengeti! We'll take in Lake Albert, and then fly up here to Murchison Falls."

Mary looked at the pilot. "Is it safe?"

He laughed. "I beg your pardon?"

*   *   *

The small plane flew low over the river, its contour reflected on the water. Along the banks were elephants, buffalo, and hippopotami. Mary sat in the co-pilot's seat, taking pictures with a small camera. Ernest sat behind the pilot so that he could see from either side. The pilot took the plane lower, lower, until they were skimming the tops of the trees.

Suddenly a telegraph wire appeared. The pilot swerved, too late. The wire caught the propeller and tail unit. Weaving crazily, the plane began to fall. Curving away from the river, it went into a nosedive and disappeared behind a wood of shrubs and small trees. There was the sound of a crash, then a weird, disturbing silence.

Within twenty-four hours, word of the crash was broadcast on U.S. television. The announcer was grave.

"Ernest Hemingway, one of the century's most well known American writers, has died in a plane crash in East Africa. He was fifty-five years old. Hemingway, who received the Pulitzer Prize, was decorated many times for his wartime contributions—"

Just then a page was placed on the announcer's desk. He picked it up, scanned it, then read aloud the news update.

"Hemingway's alive! He survived the plane crash and then there was a second plane crash while they were trying to fly him out of the wilderness! Right now he's in the New Stanley Hotel, badly hurt. Reports say he's drinking gin by the quart, reading the premature obituaries with indecent pleasure. He's insisting on his invulnerability and telling reporters he's never felt better in his whole life."

Others in the television studio began to clap.

"He's still hovering between life and death. Serious concussion, puncturing of the liver, spleen, and kidney, temporary loss of eyesight in the left eye, loss of hearing in the left ear, contusion of the spine, sprained right arm, right shoulder and left leg, first degree burns on his face, arms and head . . ."

Ketchum—Spring, 1961

Ernest sat in front of the large window in the living room of their house, staring out at the bend in the Big

Wood River. The river was lined on both sides by high aspens and Canadian poplars. A narrow gravel driveway led from the house down to a bridge over the train tracks.

A car came up the driveway and stopped. Two men, curiosity seekers, stared at the house. Ernest squeezed his eyes together, then turned away. He went to the door with unsure, hesitant steps.

"Mary!"

She came downstairs. "What is it, Papa?"

"They're here again. They're going to arrest me. Look."

She opened the door and looked out. The car was gone.

"Nonsense. It was probably some tourists. You know how they are."

"Sheriff's after me, Mary."

"Ernest, it's all in your head."

She went to his writing table, took out a package of paper, and put a sheet on the desk. "Write something, dear," she said. "Just write and you'll forget all about the things that worry you."

He tried to write. He tore up the page, began another. He read aloud. "While I watched on television, I was sure that our president will be able to deal with the heated atmosphere of our times."

He ripped the paper up and began again.

"In such hard times as these, both for our country and the world, it is good—"

He dropped back into the chair. Rubbing his hands over his face, he began to cry.

* * *

In his plaid cap and heavy boots, Ernest walked slowly along the main street of Ketchum, kicking a can. He saw some children playing in a school yard and waved to them. He waved to people across the street. He waved to his reflection in a shop window.

Mary waited in the Lincoln, parked at the intersection. Ernest got in without saying a word. As she eased the big car from the parking space her fender nicked a car parked on her left.

"Stop the car!" shouted Ernest.

"It's nothing, dear."

Ernest got out, looked back at her. "Do you want the sheriff to arrest me?" he demanded. He took out a pad and pencil, wrote down the car's license number. As he was writing, the car's owner approached him. Together they looked at the car. There was no trace, not even a scratch.

"Nothing to worry about," said the owner. "Everything's fine."

Ernest tore off a sheet of paper, handed it to him. "Just in case," he said. "Here's my address. Please take it. Okay? You can call me if you want. In case the sheriff has any questions. Okay?"

He got back in the car and sat down next to Mary. As she drove up the street, he continued to look around anxiously, as though they were being followed.

* * *

Later in the week Ernest woke late and went to his desk to write. He was alone. He arranged and rearranged all his papers. He picked up a manuscript page, put it down. He wrote something on a blank page and tore it up.

Loaded with grocery bags, Mary came in by the back door. She was in a good mood as she put away the things she'd bought.

She came out of the kitchen and went into the hall. She stopped, as though riveted to the spot. Ernest stood in a corner of the living room by the gun rack, wearing the same red bathrobe Mary had embroidered for him in Italy. He was holding a bolt-action hunting rifle. Lying close by on the windowsill were two cartridges. Mary took a deep breath and spoke quietly.

"Ernest, Dr. Saviers will be here soon," she said. "He wants to take your blood pressure."

Ernest said nothing.

Still trying to make light of the situation, Mary took off her jacket and hung it up, as if everything were normal.

"You were writing, dear. Did you make any progress?"

He stood there, motionless. In his hand was a slip of paper, covered with scrawled figures. He put it in his bathrobe pocket.

"Don't worry, dear," she said from a distance. "The writing will come back. You have so much to say, so many stories. You're still the champ. You'll show them all."

She heard the doctor's tires on the gravel driveway. Relieved, she ran to the kitchen, opened the door, and let him in.

Dr. Saviers saw Ernest and grasped the situation immediately. He put his bag on the table and took out his blood pressure gauge. Then he crossed the room to Ernest and took the rifle out of his hands. He led him to the machine, made him sit down.

"I can't write," said Ernest. "It just won't come." There were tears rolling down his cheeks. The doctor helped him walk across the room. He lay on the couch and closed his eyes.

In the kitchen the doctor spoke quietly to Mary. "I'm only a country doctor, Mary," he said. "But this much I know: Ernest needs help urgently. I can't give it to him. His condition is very serious, and it's so far outside my experience that I can't even diagnose it. He has to go to a special clinic. Right away. I'll go with you."

A short time later they were all in the car, headed for the clinic. Ernest, sitting in the back, looked out the window at the countryside. He was humming, trying to recall a melody.

"I can't get it," he said.

"What?" Mary inquired.

"The song. The way it goes."

"What song?"

Ernest stared at his hands, then looked at her. "I can't remember."

They stopped in a service station for gas. There was a small general goods store across the street. Ernest noticed it, smiled, and spoke to Mary in a normal voice.

"I'm going to run over there and get some things for breakfast. A few apples, cheese. You want some mixed pickles?"

She nodded. He left the car, crossed the street, and went into the general store. When a salesman approached, Ernest asked to see the Springfield hunting rifle displayed on the rear wall. The salesman handed it to him.

"I'll bet you're a good shot, Mr. Hemingway. I'll bet you're as good as your father."

Amazed, Ernest looked at him. "Did you know my father?"

The salesman smiled and shook his head. "Not personally," he said. "I just know what you wrote about him. You see, I'm a great fan of yours."

The salesman went into a back room and returned with a stack of books. He put them down in front of Ernest, who scanned the titles: *In Our Time*, *Winner Take Nothing*, *The Sun Also Rises*, *A Farewell to Arms*, *Death in the Afternoon*, *The Torrents of Spring*, *Men Without Women*, *For Whom the Bell Tolls*, *Across the River and Into the Trees*, *The Old Man and the Sea*. Moved, Ernest looked through them.

"All first editions," he said.

The salesman nodded proudly. "You must have loved your father very much from the way you write about him."

"He was a great hunter," Ernest said. "He had

wonderful eyes. He could see like an eagle. When I was eleven he gave me my first rifle and three cartridges a day. I was only allowed to shoot what I could eat by myself. Once I shot a porcupine. He made me eat it."

"Tell me," said the salesman. "You write wonderful short stories. What's the shortest story you ever heard?"

Ernest thought for a moment. "It was a classified ad in the newspaper. It said, 'For sale—one pair of baby shoes—never used.'"

When Mary came to get him, Ernest was seated at a table, carefully signing each of the first editions. When he was finished, she took his arm and they left.

* * *

The following day Mary was called into the office of the clinic's resident physician. The doctor studied a list of test results.

"We've given your husband a very thorough checkup, Mrs. Hemingway," he said. "The good news is that most of the tests and lab reports give us every reason to be optimistic. We're confident that we'll not only be able to diagnose Mr. Hemingway's condition, but that we'll also be able to cure him."

Mary breathed a sigh of relief. The doctor continued.

"With the exception of high blood pressure, all the organic tests were essentially negative. The blood sugar level indicates a slight diabetes mellitus. His present weight of 174 pounds is ideal. We found a swelling on the left side of his liver. The diabetes symptom and the enlarged liver are probably the results of longtime alcohol consumption. We believe that your husband may possibly have hematosis, a very rare disease. The final diagnosis will have to await a biopsy."

"What about his mood swings, the depressions?"

"We believe the depression is a result of the medication he's been taking to subdue hypertonia. But the depression is very serious. That's why we've decided to treat him with electroshock therapy."

He gave her a form to sign. "You needn't worry, Mrs. Hemingway. The patient is asleep during treatment. It only takes a few minutes. Think of it this way: The electricity disturbs the brain patterns that are causing the psychopathic behavior. It enables the healthy patterns to take over. The same way you erase magnetic tape."

The same day Ernest was given his first electroconvulsion. As they put the needle to his arm he began to dream. Suddenly, from the blackness, came a light. It was the sun and it was shining down on him and his father. Ernest was six years old and they were fishing from a rowboat. Ernest got a hit.

"Bring him in," said his father, handing him the oars.

"I will, Dad, I will!" Ernest braced his feet and reeled in.

"You're doing, wonderfully, Son. I think he's coming!"

Ernest fought the fish. His father got the net ready. Drawing it through the water, he snatched up an enormous pike.

The dream dimmed, changed. They were on their way back to the house when they saw a large fire burning outside. Ernest's mother appeared, wearing a housedress and carrying a large tray with snakes and amphibians in jars, preserved by formaldehyde. She put it on the ground beside some small stuffed animals. She began throwing the things, one by one, into the fire.

"I found all this plunder up in the attic," she said to his father. "The fire's the best place for this old stuff. It's worthless."

"But, Mama," cried Ernest. "That's Daddy's collection!"

"You hush up," she said. "It's none of your business."

Ernest looked up at his father, who lowered his gaze. Without a word he turned and went into the house, his shoulders slumped.

Furious and disappointed, Ernest began to cry. Everything went black.

* * *

Several weeks later Ernest lay in bed, his hair in disarray, hanging over his forehead. He looked years older to Mary, who sat in a chair beside his bed. The physician was trying to put him at ease.

"It's all in your imagination, Mr. Hemingway," he said.

Ernest shook his head. "I know very well the FBI is after me. When can I go home?"

"When you promise not to commit suicide."

"I promise I'll try not to."

When the doctor had gone, Ernest turned to Mary. "Did they follow you?" he asked.

"Nobody followed me, Ernest."

"The FBI's relentless! I paid my taxes. What do they want me for?"

"They're not after you."

"It's because I lived in Havana! Because I'm Castro's friend. I donated my Nobel Prize to the Cubans, I kissed their flag. Have I beat the cancer?"

"You don't have cancer, Papa."

"That's what they tell you."

Mary took two telegrams from her bag and read them to her husband. "From Dos Passos in Baltimore: 'Hem, hope you don't get too used to it there. Take it easy, good luck, Dos.' And here's one from Gary Cooper and his wife: 'What can we say except know that we love you.'"

Ernest made no reaction. "They're destroying my brain, Mary. My memory. The most valuable thing I possess. I won't be able to work." He looked Mary straight in the eyes. "An excellent treatment, but unfortunately we've lost the patient."

* * *

A few weeks later they were home in their comfortable house in Ketchum. Ernest stood at the window looking outside. Mary sat by the fire. He spoke to her in a soft but decisive and factual voice.

"The doctors just say no to everything. No more eating what I want. No more drinking. No more hunting, no more mountain climbing. If I can't live the way I want . . ."

"I love you, Papa," Mary said simply.

He turned and looked at her, smiling. "I know. You're very good to me, Kitten. But I've always lived a certain way. And I can't live any other way."

She went to him, put her arms around him tenderly. "It's going to be all right," she said. "Everything's going to be all right."

* * *

The next morning Ernest, wearing his red bathrobe, came quietly down the carpeted stairs. The first of the day's rays lay speckled on the living room floor. Ernest took a small bunch of keys from the windowsill over the kitchen sink, opened the cellar door, and went downstairs. He unlocked a small storage room.

From his collection of guns he selected a Boss shotgun. He put two shells in his pocket and went upstairs to the hallway. He took the two shells and loaded the gun expertly and without haste. He placed the butt on the floor. Leaning forward, he placed the two barrels against his forehead, just above his eyes.

He squeezed the trigger.